Roberto Travagliante

WORDPRESS
from "A" to ""

The definitive guide you need to give life to your blog,
secrets and tools to make it grow, achieving success.

"Test of a program can be used to show the presence of bugs, but never to show their absence."

Edsger Wybe Dijkstra - Structured programming, 1972

This book is dedicated to my sweet little princess and to the other half of myself, my wife. She has always believed in me, even if what I was doing did not seem to respect the canons of normality and rationality.

Contents

Preamble

What is a blog? The first time I posed this question, I was on holiday, sitting on the beach at two meters from the sea, with the girl who would become, in a few months, the woman of my life.

The sky was clear, there was a smell of salt air that can be felt near the shoreline and the climate that I have the pleasure of living for 10, maximum 15 days a year, dreaming it for the remaining 350, during which I usually live in a very cold city.

Someone is asking: *"OK, but I bought a book on blogging and WordPress. Why this woman is significant about this book?"*.

Well, her presence is crucial, because she was the first person that made me think about the possibility to enter the wonderful world of blogging, by creating my own blog.

Thanks to her, at the end of August, in 2007, my first blog "Space 4 Tutorial" (http://www.space4tutorial.com/) was born.

On that day a wonderful experience began and I got great satisfaction, over the years, both personally and professionally.

I'm working in the computer industry for over ten years. I started working as a developer of web applications concerning branch banking and now I deal with both programming and administration of operating systems and networking.

But if I had not the luck to hear a sentence (probably said randomly) by the woman who is my wife today, I'm not sure things would have been the same. Maybe now I would not be here talking about blogs.

On January 1, 2008 was the time of the portal named "Il Bloggatore" (http://www.ilbloggatore.com/). It was born from the blogger experience that I gained in the previous months and from the desire to give my contribution, even if minimally, to the Italian blogosphere improvement, by providing an absolutely free service offering support and promotion of blogs related to information technology.

Thanks to "Il Bloggatore", I was able to discover and overcome many of the challenges inherent in the creation of a blog and its subsequent growth. In fact, the development of a portal like this one, that became quickly an important reference point for much of the Italian bloggers working in this context, has enabled me to learn many aspects that a new blogger has to deal, from the earliest instants he decides to take this road.

Moreover, thanks to this website, I personally experienced all of those suggestions, apparently only theoretical. Many of them can be read on the Internet, and are related to quality of contents, indexing of a web site and presence in search engine's results, if possible on the first page.

For example, I can say with knowledge of the facts that from the appropriate use of SEO techniques depends the greater or lesser visibility of a website and, consequently, its higher success. I still remember the day when, during December of 2008, a modification to the graphical structure of the portal, seemingly small, allowed to "Il Bloggatore" nearly double the number of users who visited it daily.

Today, after more than 4 years, "Il Bloggatore" is a website that can rely on a good popularity in Italy, a PageRank of 6/10 and over a million visits per month.

If you do not know what is the PageRank, you can find more information under "Essential Concepts and Definitions" of the first chapter of this book. For the moment, however, we can consider that the Microsoft website in Italy (http://www.microsoft.it) has PageRank 7/10.

So, I guess you can understand my great satisfaction!

"Il Bloggatore" is the reference website for over 3,000 Italian blogs, originally specialized in computer, but now also projected to other topics. It tries to improve every day, providing the most effective support possible for all bloggers who need it.

In this period, almost five years since that August of 2007, I was able to discover so many things, not only about the world of blogging, but also concerning the management of websites in general.

I discovered, for example, the use of CMS (Content Management Systems), useful tools available to any webmaster, as well as optimization techniques defined as SEO (Search Engine Optimization), the methods to write quality and attractive posts, the methods to publicize your own work and "make a name" on the Internet, to make money with an Internet business, and so on...

In short, I would have lost many of these things, if I had never taken the road of blogging!

This is why I decided to create this book. Because I want to share with everyone all the things that I learned during this wonderful experience allowing, even to those who do not know what is a blog, to create one by their own and, above all, to obtain the same satisfaction that I had.

Although the topic is very extensive, this book will deal in a more complete and comprehensive as possible all aspects pertaining to the realm of blogging, especially referring to WordPress, one of the platforms on development of blogs that in recent years got the most success.

For whom is this book intended? Well, I think this book is for everyone!

In fact, the main goal of this book is to support the person that comes close to this topic just today and that one who wants to challenge himself for the first time in the creation of his own blog (development of specific web space to be submitted to friends and relatives, implementation of a simple website for business, etc.).

Moreover, this book wants to become a useful reference guide for more experienced reader or for the most seasoned webmaster, who can derive useful insights, undertake new initiatives in his own personal and professional activities and obtain new inputs, necessary to enter fully and without restrictions in a market ever more rich of opportunities that are just waiting to be discovered and exploited. In any case, whether you're a novice or an experienced webmaster, I wish you a pleasant reading, with the hope that the world of blogging will conquer you as it has conquered me some years ago.

Chapter 1 - Introduction

Blog: who is this?

Before getting to the heart of topic, we start to answer the initial question specified in the preamble: what is a blog?

Usually a blog is defined as a web service by which you can share with others your own thoughts and your opinions in a sort of *"virtual diary"*.

If we read the meaning of the word *"blog"* on the Wikipedia free encyclopedia, we find: *"... a blog is a website, usually maintained by an individual or an entity where the author (blogger) publishes periodically, as in a sort of online diary, thoughts, opinions, and other considerations, along with other types of electronic equipment such as images or video"*.

In fact, usually a blog is considered as a diary. Not surprisingly, the word *"blog"* comes from a contraction of the words *"web"* and *"log"* to *"weblog"* (*"diary on the web")*.

The term *"weblog"* dates from 1997, while its truncated version, *"blog"* was introduced for the first time by Peter Merholz, who in 1999 used the phrase *"we blog"*, thus coining a new verb *"to blog"*.

So, the main feature of a blog is to allow the sharing of information of various kinds and format, providing an important tool to show the right to freedom of thought, also over the Internet.

But a blog is not just this thing. A blog is also a medium that allows bloggers to get in touch with their readers, giving them the opportunity to express their ideas on the topics covered and, more generally, about the contents.

I think this is the aspect that makes the blog a much more exciting than any other type of service on the web. In fact, using a blog, readers have the opportunity to deal with blogger and back, through the system of "comments", which we will see in more detail in Chapter 7.

Traditional Websites, Forums and Blogs

So, a blog is nothing more than a website. Then, why can not we just call it "Website"? What makes it different than a traditional website? O compared to a forum, for example?

I am convinced that the main difference lies in the mode of interaction between the webmaster and / or the blogger and its users / readers.

To better understand this, we start by analyzing a traditional site. In a traditional website, the webmaster prepares a structure (for example, he develops the HTML pages) and uploads the contents (texts, images and other multimedia content, and so on...).

Once that is done, he has no means of interaction with its readers, through the website unless it draws up a special mask for contacts to be used to receive messages that actually get delivered by an e-mail address.

Obviously, this system moves a possible dialogue between the webmaster and its users on another channel, for example the e-mail.

In the past, because of the need to have a closer and immediate dialogue, many webmasters have shifted their focus on forums.

In fact, forums allowed a very direct relationship between the various users who attended them and, therefore, they allow the webmasters that, for example, developed company websites, to communicate with their customers, to better understand their needs, to offer them post-sales support, and so on...

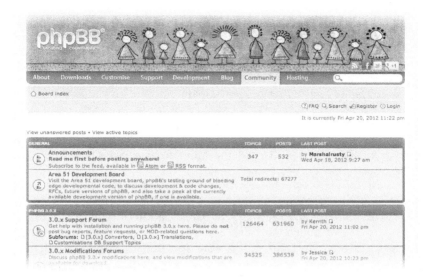

However, the solution offered by the forum, although the one hand allows users to communicate, interact and collaborate with the webmaster and, more generally, with the managers and / or moderators, it has some other critical elements which, in my opinion, should not be ignored:

1) usually, to launch a forum, you need to have registered users that become members and that access through a username and password;

2) It is extremely difficult to start a forum, without having a good number of active users.

Regarding the first point, imagine you landing for the first time on a forum, thanks to research done by the search engine for excellence: Google.

How much are you prepared to make a registration process and to complete access to a forum that you are visiting for the first time?

My own experience has shown me that very few people agree to join a forum, the first time they visit it. Most users choose to register on a forum only if the content is extremely interesting, and then if it is useful to intervene in different discussions or, alternatively, if they need help and / or assistance regarding a particular topic.

This, because most users generally use the Internet as a reference tool, with the purpose of obtaining information, rather than a willingness to actively participate in the formation of the information.

Instead, about the second aspect, it should be emphasized that the ability of a forum to attract new members and grow, paradoxically depends also on the number of active users, the same who already participate in it.

In fact, a new visitor, who is a potential user but not yet a member, will be more inclined to intervene in a discussion forum where he immediately feels a great participation of other members.

To better understand this aspect, let's imagine again to take a drink with a friend and to be able to choose between two pubs located on the same street or in the same square. Where we will go, more likely? I believe in the most crowded.

It may seem less obvious choice, because maybe we have to queue and wait a few more minutes to be served. But the motivation that drives us to make our choice is the fact that if there are more people, coffee is probably most delicious, or service is better, or manager is more friendly, and so on...

Well, in a forum, the situation is identical. A forum where there are active users on most topics and where there are well developed discussions by several members (very large threads), definitely becomes much more appealing than a forum in which participation is lower, both in terms of quantity and quality.

That's why it is very difficult to start up a forum, without good basis in terms of potential members. To overcome this difficulty, when someone asks me a tip on this, I suggest starting first with the creation of a website and / or blog to attract visitors and get to know their tastes and motivations that drive them to consult the site. And I recommend to open the forum only when he can count on a good number of potential members.

Maybe right now you are asking yourself: "Yes, but I wanted to read a book about blogs. Why we are talking about forum?". Because from analysis of these issues arises the need to create a blog!

In fact, as we said, traditional websites do not allow a good interaction with users, while the forum, since they are based entirely on this interaction, are not easy to start and maintain, and often do not lead to desired results.

So, here is the usefulness of the blog, which solves our problems!

A blog has the normal appearance of a traditional site, with the potential of interaction similar to those of a forum. However, it does not have the defects already mentioned, regarding the forum.

In fact, the blog allows you to provide information (the same content that would be present on a traditional site) and to open a discussion about such content, using an important comment system, allowing all users to intervene, expressing their own opinions, thoughts, etc.

This can happen more or less freely, according to the rules established by the bloggers, who can choose to moderate comments or not, as well as to force users to register or not. But these issues are best analyzed in Chapter 7, dedicated to the comment system.

At the time, you need to know that the participation of users, is important but not essential to the success of a blog.

In fact, on the Internet there are blogs where comments are open to everyone, in the best spirit of sharing and greater freedom of expression and thought.

But there are also blogs that do not give users any opportunity to comment on the articles contained therein, except upon subscription and authentication. In the latter case, blogs assume a function of pure consultation of contents, by visitors.

However, participation is certainly one of the main reasons why blogs had a major impact on the area of information, becoming, to date, one of the most important tools about online communication.

Why decide to create a blog?

What pushes a person, an institution and / or a company to create a blog?

The reasons are many and very different from each other. You can start a blog just to share your thoughts, your moods, your point of view about most different topics . In this case, the blog assumes a very personal character and it very often becomes a "safety valve" for blogger, who uses it as a real diary.

The category of personal blogs is very common. In a blog of this kind, usually you can find comments left by friends and / or occasional visitors.

But this is not the only type of blog. In fact, next to personal blogs, we find, for example, corporate blogs, created for sponsorship and / or promotion of products and services, or for customer support.

This kind of blog is often used to provide the company a direct connection to its customers. Indeed, through a corporate blog, it is possible to know the tastes of customers, the problems encountered during the use of certain products, the opinions, and so on.

At other times, blogs are created with the intention of creating centers for aggregation for people who share opinions, hobbies, and so on...

The "collective blogs" and the "social blogs" are very common categories of blog. The first type is characterized by the blogs in which web content is created and uploaded by a more or less limited group of authors, usually with specific interests. The social blogs, instead, are characterized by the fact of being open and accessible to everyone. In these blogs, all users who are registered can publish articles.

However, regardless of the type of blog you want to achieve, the goal of this book is to guide you in detail the various phases that regard its creation and its development, and to provide you with any useful suggestions for its growth and full achievement of your goals.

Essential Concepts and Definitions

Before delving into various aspects relating to the creation of a blog, we see some brief definition that can be useful in the hereafter, and that, eventually, we will review in more detail in next chapters.

Advertiser - in an advertising system, who promotes its products or services through online advertising, in the spaces provided on websites, by the Publisher.

Blog - contraction of "weblog" - website, usually maintained by one person or a group of persons (possibly by a company or institution), where the author (blogger) publishes periodically its thoughts, opinions, and other considerations, by using, where appropriate, other types of electronic material, such as pictures or videos.

Browser - software by which you can access several websites on the Internet and browse the relevant pages and their contents. Examples of browsers are "Microsoft Internet Explorer", "Mozilla Firefox", "Apple Safari", "Google Chrome", or "Opera Browser".

CMS - (Content Management System) - software system, installed on a web server and designed to easily provide management for website contents, freeing the webmaster by the need to know the languages and web programming techniques.

Database - the set of files and archives organized in a particular logical structure, for the management of data on which you can perform different actions (insert, search, edit and delete).

DBMS - (DataBase Management System) - software system for creating and managing databases, usually intended for use by multiple users.

DNS - (Domain Name System) - system for resolving domain names. Specifically, the DNS is the service that takes care of converting domain names (such as www.blogname.com) to their IP addresses, codes consisting of 4 numbers (octets) that uniquely identify each host on Internet network (TCP / IP).

FTP - (File Transfer Protocol) - protocol used for the transfer of files from one host to another, in a TCP / IP network such as Internet.

Hosting - service that allows an operator (Internet Service Provider), to provide a user (in our case, the blogger) a web server to host pages of a web site (or, more specifically, a blog).

HTML - (HyperText Markup Language) tag-based language for text formatting, used for the representation of hypertext contents which must be inserted in the pages of a web site.

HTTP - (HyperText Transfer Protocol) - protocol used for transferring hypertext documents from one host to another (such as web pages). Today is the most common protocol used on the Internet and allows the normal navigation between different web sites present in the world.

ISP - (Internet Service Provider) - A company that provides Internet services, such as email, web space, etc.

ICT - (Information and Communication Technology) - the set of methods and technologies for the realization of systems of transmission, reception and processing of information (including digital technologies).

Layout - layout and graphic structure of a web site or document, with particular reference to the provision of text, images, etc.

MySQL - free and open sources DBMS, used for database management, characterized by great flexibility and efficiency, and much used in the creation of Web applications, in conjunction with PHP.

Page Rank - It is an algorithm, patented by Stanford University, which allows you to assign a numerical score to one or more hyperlinks, to indicate their importance and popularity. Typically, when we talk about Page Rank, we refer to an index that defines the popularity of a web page or entire website. This indicator of popularity, is one of the elements that underlie the search engines into the results. In particular, sites with higher page rank are shown before the others, in searches.

PHP - scripting language widely used for programming and developing applications for the Web.

Publisher - in an advertising system, who provides space on a blog and, more generally, on a website to advertise products or services sold by Advertiser.

SEO - (Search Engine Optimization) - The set of optimization techniques that will achieve the best positioning of a website, regarding the search engines. It includes all activities performed on the pages of a website to improve the visibility of the site itself against the search engines, increasing traffic (in terms of visits) received by them.

SQL - (Structured Query Language) - standard language for relational databases management, which allows querying, inserting and updating data, and the cancellation.

URL - (Universal Resource Locator) - alphanumeric string that uniquely identifies a resource on the Internet, as a document, image, video, music file, etc. The following is the typical structure of a URL: *protocol://<username:password@>host<:port></path><?querystring><#anchor>*. Samples of URL are: http://www.space4tutorial.com, mailto:info@space4tutorial.com, ftp://rtravagliante:password@myserver/directoryftp/.

Web server - server (or service) where, using special software, the pages of a web site are provided. These pages may be accessed by users, through a special program, known as "browser".

Wordpress - CMS oriented in creation of blog, based on PHP language and on MySQL DBMS.

Chapter 2 - Not Only WordPress

The blogging platforms

If you're reading this book, of course, you're interested in using WordPress to create your blog. However, it should be emphasized that there is not only WordPress and that a blog can be made in many other ways and with many tools.

In particular, in recent years, many blogging services have emerged, both free and paid, each with their strengths and their weaknesses. They might be a good solution for those want to create their own blog easily with a few clicks.

Among the most important ones, active not only in Italy, must surely be counted the following:

- Blogger;
- Wordpress.com (hosting platform, It should not be confused with WordPress.org, website from which you can download the software having the same name);
- Splinder (officially closed January 31, 2012);
- Myspace;
- Windows Live Spaces.

Obviously, this list is not exhaustive, these are just the most common platforms.

However, it should be emphasized that a blog created using these services may have limitations compared to the potential of another one created by using WordPress on your own hosting service. This, of course, always related to the needs of the blogger.

In fact, when you decide on a blogging service like this, it may happen that some activities (for example, those related to customizing graphics) are sometimes limited to a selection of layouts and / or templates from a variety of already designed models on which you can only insert your own image to use it as a header and / or background.

Nevertheless, some people may consider sufficient to create a blog unpretentious. In this case, the blogging platforms mentioned may be the best solution that best suits your needs.

WordPress.org or WordPress.com?

Among the different blogging services, we have quoted WordPress.com.

This service provides the ability to create a blog with WordPress, in a few clicks and, if so desired, without the need to provide for the purchase of a hosting plan and space where you can install the software WordPress.

Instead, WordPress.org is the site from which you can download the WordPress software product. This software must be installed and configured on our web space.

As already said, a free blog on WordPress.com has several limitations, especially about the possibility to install new graphic templates and new plugins. So, I suggest you to download the .ZIP or TAR.GZ format for WordPress archive, from WordPress.org website, and immediately choose a specific hosting plan for the blog, along with registration of a new domain name as www.blogname.com.

Don't worry, this type of installation is not complicated and in the following pages we will learn how to prepare a typical configuration of WordPress, directly on our web space!

Static and dynamic sites: The importance of CMS

Until not long ago and still today, for many websites, webmasters were forced to intervene in a widespread manner on the code of various web pages.

Therefore, to publish something on the Internet, was necessary to know languages such as HTML, PHP, and so on, or to rely on some expert who knew them well enough.

Whenever it was necessary to make some changes to the website, it was necessary to work fairly complex update, and for this reason, it was essential to have the right expertise and experience Furthermore, in terms of time and energy, the maintenance of the site became more expensive than the first realization.

Many people and / or companies, in conclusion, abandoned their websites themselves, with severe discomfort for visitors who found outdated information on them.

Gradually, the need to simplify this task of updating, especially regarding the informative contents, rather than structural aspects, has led to design and develop software solutions to facilitate website management.

Thus, CMS has begun to spread.

A CMS (Content Management System) is a software tool installed on a web server and created for loading, editing, deleting, and, more generally, manage information made available on a website. It's important to point out that most of the CMS, once installed and configured, can help manage an entire website, even by those without technical knowledge of web programming.

A CMS allows you to manage a website in a completely dynamic mode, generally through the use of a database, containing, in addition to some aspects related to its configuration, information to be made available to visitors of the website itself.

In addition, many CMS also allows you to manage various aspects of the structure of the website, such as the layout, the mode of information representation and so on, and to enable access by multiple users via web interfaces that make up the so-called back-office site.

Currently, on the market there are several types of CMS to build websites of all kinds. In particular, focusing our attention on blogs, we can choose products as "Joomla!" (Created especially for the realization of large portals), "Movable Type", "Nucleus CMS", "Textpattern", "dBlog" and many more.

Certainly, however, the most popular platform for the creation of blogs appears to be "WordPress".

WordPress

WordPress is a CMS based on PHP scripting language with a MySQL database It was created by Matt Mullenweg and is released under the GNU General Public License, which allows its distribution and its use free and open.

Wordpress has the following main features, which make it a key product about the realization of a blog:

- it is a free product, available free of charge and without license fees;
- it is an open-sources software and, therefore, you can make changes and improvements to the PHP code to fit your needs;
- On the Internet there is a wide availability of ready-made graphic templates, to customize your blog;
- There is a large supply of ready-made add-ons (plugins), which help integrate new features, not found in the basic package.

Also, the following additional strengths should not be underestimated:

- the ability to organize contents into categories;
- the possibility of use by several authors;
- optimization of URL into permalinks to improve its presence on search engines;

- pingback functions (we will see better what they are in Chapter 7, dedicated to participation of readers and to comment system);
- creation of static pages;
- writing content with a comfortable visual editor.

It should be emphasized that, even if on one side the fact of relying on a relational database allows in principle to use any other DBMS, on the other hand it is preferable to use MySQL, to achieve the improved stability and compatibility with the various components of WordPress itself, as well as with the various additional components that can be installed.

The importance of database

Generally, the pages of a website on which a CMS like WordPress is running, are built dynamically, based on the content in a database and previously uploaded by the users.

In practice, when a user opens a page of the site and / or blog, CMS shows this page using predetermined graphic structure, generated by a model or template, and filling it with datas obtained from the database (the information that was previously loaded from operator of the site).

Examples of this information is the page title, body, author, creation date, etc.

In this perspective, the database is of fundamental importance in the management of the site, as it represents the place where you find the information made available to readers of a site.

This consideration is important when choosing the web space where the blog must be hosted.

In fact, very often we can see hosting offerings that attract customers by making available hundreds of megabytes or several gigabytes of web space, but they may not provide services as database management, or they provide them only as "extras", at additional cost also very high.

So, you must pay attention when you choose the hosting plan for your blog, carefully evaluating this aspect.

Chapter 3 - Before you start

The choice of main topic

The first step to take, before you create a new blog, is the choice of main topic (or topics, if they are more than one) you want to be discussed on it.

All this may seem obvious, but it very often happens that you create a blog without having a clear idea of the purposes that the same should have and the issues to be addressed.

From this point of view, a very common mistake is to identify a reference material (a "niche", to use a term that web marketing experts like) too wide, which does not allows the blog to develop into effectively.

Indeed, a consideration that you can't usually found in manuals, but that comes with experience and common sense, is that if the niche is saturated and large, it will take more time and more work to grow the blog.

Moreover, if the topics discussed are extensive, it will be extremely difficult to write quality articles that address all aspects in depth.

Consequently, the blog will not be considered worthy of attention, and even users who visit it by chance, will not find interesting contents (you will not have the so-called "conversion") and immediately leave the blog.

Let's take an example: as a blogger, I might decide to create a blog that covers the computer topics at 360 degrees, or I could opt for a blog that features the only programming for mobile devices (for example: Apple iOS, Google Android, or Microsoft Windows phone).

Obviously, in the first case I'm free to deal with any topic of computer, both related to the programming and system administration, or related to the graphics, or safety of telecommunications, and so on....

However, the first problem that would occur would be to create structure with many menus and very complex sections, to handle all matters related to ICT (Information and Communication Technology).

Not to mention that, to create a blog for quality, you should post informative content on various topics, or you risk creating a blog full of gaps, which contains no the detailed information that it intends to have.

Instead, by choosing a well bounded niche, we can address each argument in a more comprehensive, easily conquering our users, who'll find in ourselves and in our blog a reference point.

Furthermore, it is necessary to evaluate the level of saturation in certain niches. In fact, there are million of blogs dedicated to mobile phones it is normal to wonder why a visitor should choose our blog over another.

In contrast, a blog about, for example, the sole reviews of PC games, or computer security tutorials, or exclusively guides on graphic products, may be more attractive, because of the greater level of detail.

There are also other important issues to consider, in the choice of the blog topic.

For example, it is important to ensure that competition is not too high, that is to say that there are many blogs that already face the same issues that we want to treat.

Furthermore, it is important to consider if the arguments that we propose to deal may be of interest to users and, at the same time, if we are able to write articles about the same topics, ensuring a good level in terms of competence and professionalism. This, to live our blog for the longest possible.

Enhance your interests

Unless you are not trying to create a blog for your business or company, it is important that the choice of subject is made keeping in mind the things you know well, your hobbies and interests.

In fact, if you choose topics familiar to you, you'll have more chance of success, because you know what you're talking about and, consequently, you are in a position to better interact with users that visit your blog.

For this purpose, it should be noted that it is not necessary that you know all the arguments to 100%. You just need to have the right cultural background in order to divulge good things you know and at the same time, explain what you learn during your blogging activity.

One topic or many topics?

A question I am often asked by those who intend to start blogging is this: is it more convenient to create a monothematic blog or I should develop a blog around many topics?

Well, I think the choice depends mainly from your inclinations.

We should say immediately that the realization of a multi-topic blog, from a point of view regarding only structure, is not very different from the creation of a monothematic blog.

However, we must consider that a multi-topic blog is much more complex to maintain, unless you know all the treated topics and / or you can get help by a team of bloggers.

Personally, I prefer the single-topic blogs, because they are characterized more easily, especially if they contain high quality posts, and if they represent valid points of reference for visitors, on specific topics.

This is because, consequently, visitors are more disposed to return, after first time.

Moreover, during the maintenance of a single-topic blog, the blogger has better way to specialize on a particular matter (because it has a way to learn writing, researching the information, dealing with readers, etc...), possibly becoming a "guru" and succeeding to offer a better quality support for users.

Even from the point of view of indexing by search engines, a blog that addresses issues of a specific sector is generally better, with consequent benefits in terms of positioning in the first pages of search results.

But, of course, this is just an opinion. Nothing stops you creating a successful multi-topic blog, about everything that exists "in the known Universe." However, efforts will be proportionate to the objectives to be achieved and you need careful planning on your part about activities and interventions, to make your blog successful!

The choice of the name

After choosing the topic of the blog, you need to decide the name that it should have.

It is not always easy to find a good name for your blog. This is because the name of the blog is not something that can be dealt with lightly, but it is the element that will characterize your creation forever.

Once the blog is up and online, its name can not be changed. Or better, it can be amended only by agreeing to register a new domain name.

In addition, readers will learn that the blog name and any name change, accomplished when the blog will already started, could have adverse consequences on the visits.

I know it might seem strange to many, but the name of the blog, even if a personal blog, is a bit 'as the name of a commercial product. How would you react if you find out that your favorite brand of beer has suddenly changed name?

Probably, we would think of. Personally, I would ask myself many things. Why this name has changed? Perhaps the owner has changed? maybe it's changed the company that produces it? Or worse, the production process? It will be good as always, or its quality will suffer?

It seems strange, but a name change can induce a variety of issues, some of which also unfounded, but that may discourage users of a blog, especially regulars and loyal members.

Therefore, it is preferable to choose a name immediately, with the intent to make it the final name.

How to choose the name of the blog? Well, definitely keeping in mind the main topics that will treat!

If it is a personal blog, you might think to call it by your name.

Personally, I do not feel to encourage this practice, because, although the one hand the fact of having a site bearing the our name may give us some satisfaction, the other hand it does not bring any benefit about indexing by search engine.

And, frankly, I think one of the greatest satisfactions for most bloggers is to see your blog on the first page of Google, Yahoo, or even Bing, etc.

Therefore, I suggest you to choose for a name that is most relevant to the topic treated by the blog, rather than a name that identifies the blog's author.

For example, the name of a blog that covers the computer graphics should contain the word "graphics" in it. Or, a blog about computer security, could have a name such as "security-blog.com", or "safe-to-pc.com", or "hacker-blog.org".

On many websites related blogs you can find suggestions about identifying of right keywords to be included into the site name.

To measure the better keywords you can use many tools, such as Google AdWords.

In fact, usually, you should enter the most competitive keywords in the name of the blog to be created in order to improve rankings in search engines themselves.

This can be a good idea, but keep in mind that, beyond the simple name of the blog, there must be quality contents, well written articles and search engine optimization to allow "climbing" of the SERP for certain keywords.

Leaving aside for the moment the techniques related to placement, it must be said that in some areas, especially in cases where you plan to maintain a professional writing style, but at the same time informal and playful, you can think of a name that inspires sympathy , of the type "themegagraphic.net", or "insecure-pc.com".

I remember like it was yesterday when I decided on the name of the portal of "Il Bloggatore".

I thought than a service about blogs should contain the word blog in it, but at the same time I was looking for a name that could be not "heavy", but light, a name that could be nice and that would give up the idea of what the visitor could find in it. And "Il Bloggatore" came to himself, as a voice in my mind.

That said, my personal suggestion is this: choose a name that gives the idea of what the visitor can find in your blog, eventually merge more words, but at the same time, try to form a concise name that is easy to be remembered by users.

Also, do not be hasty in deciding, choose a name that you like, because a name you like you can instill the right enthusiasm from the start and can make you proud to promote your creation.

Finally, choose a name that is easy to remember, keeping in mind that even if one side the name of a blog do not necessarily decrees its success or failure, on the other, it can be a valuable "calling card" for those who lands there for the first time, directly or through research on the Internet.

The graphics

What about graphics for your blog?

Well, we can not give a definitive answer to this question. This is because each blog is different and reflects the personality of the owner. And, like the ancient Romans used to say: De gustibus non est disputandum.

I may like the graphics of a website while you do not, and vice versa. That's the beauty of the human race!

With regard to WordPress, we must point out that on the Internet there are a myriad of graphical models (templates) that can be used in your blog.

Some of them are commercial products, while others are released under free licenses.

In the chapter 8 we will see in detail how to install a new template directly from the admin panel of WordPress.

For the moment, You just need to know that graphic design is the fundamental element on which the success or otherwise of the blog is based.

In fact, it is universally recognized that a user who surfs the Internet and lands on a website (or blog), evaluate it in an unconscious way during the first 3 to 5 seconds, deciding in this very short period of time if the site is interesting or not. Only after this period he begins to evaluate, in a conscious way, the information contained within it, starting from images, up to the reading of the text portions.

During the graphics design of a blog and, more generally, of a web site, the "layout" assumes considerable importance. In particular, graphical layout means the arrangement of several elements (menus, text, images, buttons, links, etc..) within the web page.

It is very important to prepare a suitable layout for your blog to attract visitors and keep it on the site as long as possible.

For example, it is obvious that in a web page that is full of text, without pictures and without a precise order, the visitor may tire and discourage him. This can cause his "departure" from the site. At the same time, a page that is too rich in images and moving elements (eg with too GIF animations) not organized with a certain logic, confusing the user, may cause it to escape

For these reasons, when designing the layout, you need to find the right balance between graphical and textual elements. It must be said, however, that the use of templates in WordPress makes it much easier , because you can experiment with different layouts without much effort. In many cases, we prefer to use a template and customize it based on your needs, rather than designing and developing one from scratch.

Chapter 4 - Installing WordPress

Choosing a hosting platform

Finally, after analyzing the various aspects of creating a blog, and having thought on the various factors that may affect the success or failure of our project, we are ready to give life to our "creature".

The first step is choosing the hosting platform. As mentioned in previous pages, hosting is a service that consists in an ISP (Internet Service Provider) provides us and other users, a web server, where web pages of our blog will be hosted.

Choosing the hosting plan is quite important, as the performance and the best or worst features of the blog depend from it. For this reason, the hosting plan must be chosen carefully.

First, choose a hosting plan to pay right away! The free hosting plans, although attractive, often have a number of limitations that we will notice right away, but that will prove increasingly difficult to bear, as we go into our blogging activity.

Moreover, often, choosing a hosting plan for a fee, you buy a domain name such as "blogname.com" (or .Net, .Org, etc.), whose registration costs a few dollars per year, less than a dozen, so it is worth opting for a paid service.

WordPress is a platform based on PHP scripting language and MySQL database management system. This means that our hosting plan must provide support for both PHP and MySQL.

Especially in the past, when websites were managed in a "static" mode and they did not hardly ever use of databases, hosting plans were measured depending on the amount of space available for the web pages of our site. Therefore, a provider that offered 50 MB of web space offered a service to be preferred over one that offered to 10 Mb of web space.

Today, however, the web space is no longer the only factor to consider.

In fact, if we have 10 GB of space available for web pages, but we do not have support for the management of databases, we can not use either a CMS like WordPress or one like Joomla, or other content managers that make use of databases.

So, in choosing our hosting plan, we must look for provider that includes support for .PHP pages, the larger amount of web space and, at the same time, support for MySQL, with the largest possible space for creation of databases.

In Italy and around the world, there are many Internet providers that manage hosting services. Each of them offers hosting plans with very different features, compared to others, with promotions that are constantly changing, so it's not appropriate to suggest one of them, in these pages.

This, also because the services that I used in my blogging activity with satisfaction, might not be as appropriate to your needs.

So, I'll just say that when you go looking for a hosting service for your blog, you must search through products that include:

- registration of the domain name with the suffix .COM, .IT, .EU, .NET, etc... (obviously, this is a required step if we want to create a blog with name as <www.blogname.com> or <www.blogname.net>);
- support for the PHP language;
- MySQL database management (if possible, through a comfortable web interface as that provided by PHPMyAdmin);
- FTP access to our web pages;
- possibly, the management of at least one email account "@blogname.com" (this will be useful when we decide to create a contact form to get in touch with our users);
- possibly, the direct management of our DNS (to create multiple host names, for example: www.blogname.com, forum.blogname.com, etc.)

Typically, services with these features are available for less than twenty euros per year. But, surely, if we find hosting plans at a higher price, then it does not necessarily mean that we are the victim of theft!

In fact, it may be that in addition to these features, other services will be covered, as dozens of e-mail accounts or a guaranteed bandwidth service, and so on...

These additional services may be useful or not. So, choose the platform that most convinces you! In case of problems, you can always, after a while, complete a domain transfer, handing over the hosting provider to another.

Preparing the database

From the purchase of hosting plan to domain registration and activation of the web space, generally, you can wait a few hours. About this aspect, you must note that registering domains that are very fast in the past.

Therefore, after about 24 - 48 hours, our hosting service will be active, and in most cases we will receive an email with our login information, useful to get access to the panel for the management of our space and our FTP space.

This panel will help us to manage different aspects of the service that we purchased. Generally, we will:

- create our email accounts with suffix "@blogname.com";
- edit and update information on the DNS (if necessary);
- create the database for use with WordPress.

Now, we are going to access it to create the database for use with WordPress. For correct instructions about database creation, please, read documentation provided by your ISP, because steps are different from one operator to another and, therefore, they can not be summarized in this book.

Whenever the database is created, we will get the details for access to it, via email or directly through the admin panel.

Let's take note of these data and let's start with the actual installation of WordPress.

Wordpress installation

Before starting the installation, We must say that during the following chapters, to provide all the examples and to give all the details and technical information and practical advice, we will use a specially designated web space, made available in scope of my personal domain space4tutorial.com.

In this way, each example will cover a blog that is really available on Internet, a blog that after the end of this book can be visited freely! It can be reached at the following link: http://mybook.space4tutorial.com.

Obviously, if you've already purchased your hosting service, then you can try things that we report in these pages directly on it.

That said, the initial situation is the following: we have our own hosting active, with the ability to access via FTP to the root of our website, in addition to a MySQL database running, in order to properly install and configure WordPress.

The first thing to do is download of WordPress package. Depending on our preferred language, we can use the English version, the Italian version, or other specific localized version. We can get the latest stable version of WordPress available from the global website http://wordpress.org/. The Italian version (my preferred language), however, is available through the site http://it.wordpress.org/.

To get WordPress with your preferred language, you are not obligated to download the already localized package. In fact, you can first download the English version, and then download the translation package for your preferred language. However, by downloading the already localized version in your preferred language, you avoid some unnecessary effort.

In these pages, for convenience, we will refer to the English version, because regardless of the language used, features of WordPress will be the same.

At the time of writing, the latest stable version, suitable for "production" environments (not only for test) is 3.4.1 and is available as .ZIP archive at the link http://wordpress.org/latest.zip or, as .TAR.GZ archive, at the link http://wordpress.org/latest.tar.gz.

Once you have downloaded the package into one of two formats, let's extract the archive to a folder or let's transfer its contents to FTP space made available by the hosting provider we choosed, using any FTP client.

Never heard of the FTP service?

No problem, if you've never used this service, you just know that FTP is the acronym for File Transfer Protocol. It is a service that allows the transmission of files from one computer to another, physically located in two places very distant from each other.

In particular, in our situation the FTP service will be used to transfer files extracted from the WordPress archive (.ZIP or .TAR.GZ) from our computer to the server, where we wish to install and configure our blog.

To transfer files, we generally use a software specifically designed for this function, namely an FTP client.

On internet just do a simple search to find a multitude of programs that can do the job, whether you work with Windows, or Linux, or Mac OS X.

A good FTP client for Windows and Mac, released for free, is Cyberduck.

Cyberduck is my favorite FTP software, but you can use any other application such as, for example, FileZilla, SmartFTP, Core FTP, etc..

Besides having the typical features of an FTP client, Cyberduck supports other file transfer systems, such as SFTP (FTP over SSL) and WebDAV, but we just need to transfer our files on our blog space, so we focus only use as FTP client.

Once we have downloaded the installation package from http://cyberduck.ch/ site, we can install it and go on.

Below you can see a screenshot of Cyberduck, in action on my computer:

The first thing to do is configuration of a new connection to our FTP space.

To do this, we must click on "Open Connection" and, in the form that appears, we must insert the data that we received by our hosting provider and, specifically, FTP host name, port (standard port for FTP is 21), username and password.

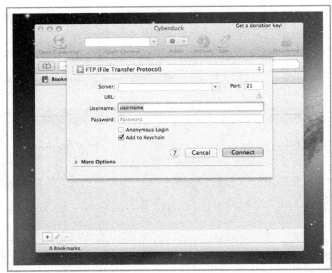

Let's click the "Connect" button and, once connected to our FTP server, let's drag all the files extracted from the WordPress window in Cyberduck, initiating the transfer of the latter within the root of our website:

When completed, we will see something very similar to the following screen, with all files copied to your WordPress blog on the web space allocated to our blog:

As we can see, the WordPress files are loaded into the root directory of the site. Up to now we simply transferred the contents of the .ZIP package (or .TAR.GZ) of WordPress.

Now we are ready to launch the installation process itself, which will set up our blog and will allow us to enter ourselves the wonderful world of blogging.

This procedure will be invoked using the browser. In fact, WordPress is a CMS oriented in management via WEB, and all future activities of installation and configuration will be done with a simple program for navigation.

If you use Microsoft Windows, then you'll most likely choose Internet Explorer, Mozilla Firefox, Google Chrome or otherwise, if we are using Linux or Mac OS X, we'll prefer respectively Mozilla Firefox or Safari browsers.

From a practical standpoint, no matter which browser we choose, we will notice no particular differences, so we'll work equally, because WordPress is, in essence, a web application and is independent of operating system used on the client side.

So, regardless of the browser we have chosen as our partner in this adventure, let's connect to our blog address: http://www.blogname.com.

In my case, I will connect to the link http://mybook.space4tutorial.com.

Since the blog is not configured yet, it appears an error page, where we are informed that file "*wp-config.php*" is missing.

The presence of this file is necessary for the proper functioning of the blog (also because it contains a whole series of information, including data for access to the database) and is checked each time a user logs on to the blog.

As this file does not exist, the installation of WordPress is asking us to create:

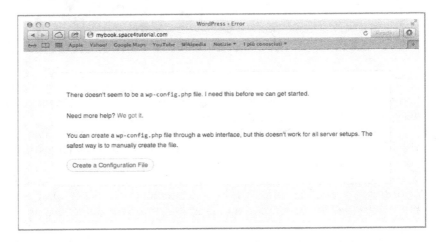

Let's click on the "Create a Configuration File" button and let's begin the installation. Here's the setup page, where we can get indication about all the necessary information to complete the installation:

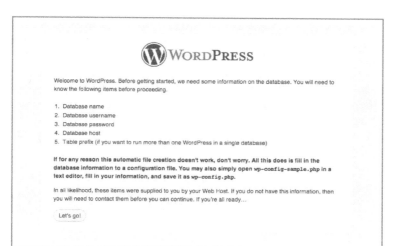

Let's click on the "Let's go!" button and let's insert the required information:

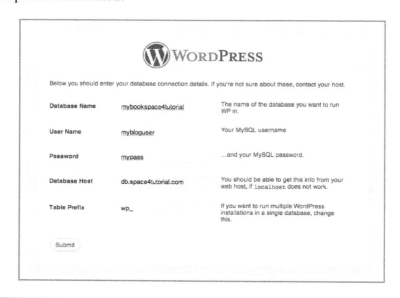

In particular, required fields are: database name (we configured it by using the admin panel of our Internet Service Provider), username, password and name of database server.

Finally, we are asked what's the prefix for tables within the database. What does it means? Well, the table prefix is the prefix that will be used in determining the names of the tables of WordPress. For example, in standard configuration, which includes the prefix "wp_", the table containing the articles of the blog will be called "wp_posts", while that with the comments "wp_comments" and so on...

This setting allows you to create multiple blogs within the same database, for example using "wp1_" for the first blog, "wp2_" for the second, and so on. Or, it can allow us to distinguish the tables of our blog from those of other web applications that use the same database.

However, in this example we let it as "wp_", which is the standard configuration, and we click on the "Submit".

If entered information is correct, WordPress will show us a page like the following:

At this time, let's click on the "Run the install" button.

We get the welcome page of WordPress, where we'll be prompted to enter other information, including the following:

- the title that we want to use for our blog;
- the username for the administrator of the blog (usually "admin");
- the administrative password (to be entered twice);

- an email address (used by WordPress, where required, to notify the administrator when new comments are written, to reset the administrative password, etc...).

In this page there is also an indication about the complexity for password that we are entering, which is useful in terms of "psychological", because we can get help in entering not simplex passwords, that may be discovered more or less randomly by some visitors.

In fact, we must keep in mind that the blog will potentially be seen by anyone in the world. And, with the increase of his reputation, after some time it will not only attract the attention of "normal" visitors, but also those of some attacker (cracker) or presumed.

In addition, we will be asked to decide, on this page, if you want make your blog visible to search engines, or not. Of course, we'll leave this option checked.

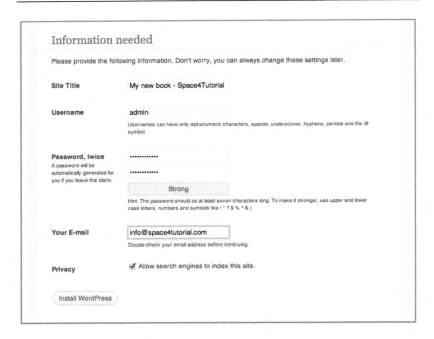

Let's click on the "Install WordPress" button. After a few seconds, we'll get confirmation that WordPress has been installed:

All right, our blog has just been installed! And we can already navigate it, by typing the appropriate link on our browser!

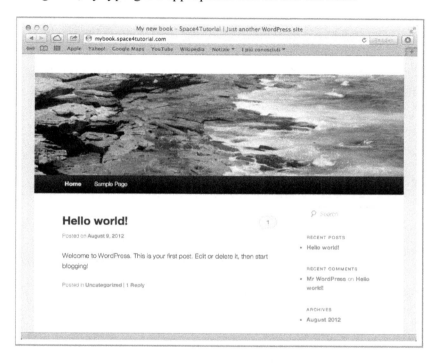

As we can see in the screenshot above, there is already a sample post, titled "Hello world!", with a test comment.

In addition, in a typical installation, WordPress also install a demo page. Both the post and the comment will be removed to make room for our content.

First login to our blog

Finally, our blog is online and it's accessible from all over the world. Now, we can begin customization and configuration of all aspects, from the graphical structure to all other elements!

To do it, we must access the administrative part of the blog, located at http://www.blogname.com/wp-admin/ (in the case of blog created in these pages, the link will be http://mybook.space4tutorial.com/wp-admin/).

Since we have not been authenticated, we get the login screen, where we will input the administrative username (default: *"admin"*) and password, configured during the first installation of our blog:

After we have clicked on the "Connect" button, we can finally access to the administration panel for our blog, more precisely the first page of it, normally known as "Dashboard":

The admin panel should be considered a bit like the "central control system" of our blog. Thanks to it, we can decide and configure all aspects related to the blog. For example, we may make the following:

- add new static pages and new posts;
- manage the comments received from users, providing for their "moderation";
- upload multimedia content such as images, video, and so on;
- manage the blog layout and interface;
- install, configure and / or remove add-ons (plugins), which permit to the blogger to expand the standard features of WordPress;
- manage users of the blog, with the ability to provide them with a separate access, according to the username and password entered;
- change the general settings of the blog;

- manage export and / or import for contents of the blog (especially useful for performing backups, or if we must complete a transfer of the blog);
- manage updates of WordPress and other software components (usually graphic templates and plugins).

In short, this admin panel is the basic tool for managing the blog, the "back-office" component that permit to us to start now, with our blogging activity.

Over the next few chapters, we will discover all of the features that this dashboard gives us, from loading of the contents that must be published in our blog, up to the management of plugins, the management of layout and interface, of users and so on.

In fact, from this moment we can organize all of the contents of our blog, by growing our own "creation" day after day. And why not, maybe we could create a truly successful blog, destined to become the reference point for many others.

The administrative panel of the blog

When we access the administration panel of WordPress, the first thing we notice is that the menu consists of several items that, especially at first, may confuse the bloggers.

However, any of these items corresponds to all the different features of the CMS in a very simple and schematic way.

At the time of of this writing, version 3.4.1 of WordPress has a two-level menu, collapsible, which means that if we need, we can reduce it dimension, to occupy the least possible space on the screen.

The main menu items, at the first level, are the following: Posts, Media, Links, Pages, Comments, Appearance, Plugins, Users, Tools and Settings. Throughout this book, they will all be analyzed, but for now we need just know that within each of these menu items, there are other submenus related to more specific functions.

Instead, on the top there is a header that contains a link useful to reach the front-end of the blog, often useful to see preview for the contents that we prepared for the blog (posts, pages, etc...).

In addition, in the header is always available the appropriate links to commonly used features, such as that relating to the approval of new comments received from readers, or uploading of new items, pages, links, etc...

Finally, on the right side of the header, we can find the options that affect the user name with which we are logging in to WordPress admin panel, like the ability to change our profile and to exit from the administration of our blog (logout).

In version 3.4.1, there are two other entries, just below the header, on the right side.

The first, "Screen Options", refers to the settings shown in the middle of the page, and the second, "Help", concerns an online guide that can provide some useful tips, especially for persons that start today to use WordPress.

In the middle of the page, instead, we can find the options for obtaining and maintaining a variety of information on the blog.

In particular, at logon, after entering the username and password, we are redirected to a particular page, called "Dashboard".

The Dashboard appears as a page consisting of several squares, each concerning a particular aspect of our blog.

In the default configuration, the following boxes are shown, in order:

- **Right now** - shows the total number of articles (or posts), pages, categories, tags (we will see what they are) and comments;
- **Recent Comments** - it allows quick access to the page containing comments, divided into approved, pending, spam and trashed;
- **Incoming Links** - it allows to view the links from other websites that are directed to our blog;
- **Plugins** - it shows the most popular plugins available on the Internet, the past developed ones and those that were recently updated;
- **QuickPress** - it allows rapid creation of a post (or article);
- **Recent draft** - it shows the latest post that are not yet published, or in "draft" state;
- **WordPress Blog** - it shows the preview of latest news, directly coming from the WordPress blog, allowing bloggers to stay tuned on topics concerning WordPress;

- **Other WordPress news** - it shows the links to latest news related to WordPress, aggregated from different web sites.

These boxes can be reduced and / or placed on the screen according to our preferences, by dragging them with the mouse (drag & drop) or removed from view, by selecting "Screen Options".

However, throughout these pages, we will leave intact the default view, because this layout organization is not "improvised", but designed to offer bloggers the best set of tools that they may need, for a quick use.

Chapter 5 - Beginning to write

Pages and Posts

In previous chapter we saw how we can easily install WordPress on our web space, so we can prepare all the necessary environment to start our blogger activity.

Specifically, we followed all the steps that relate to the first installation of this great CMS, and we created a fully functional WordPress blog, as a basis for our further work.

In this chapter, instead, we will dive into one of the most important aspects regarding the management of the blog: the web content production.

Before going ahead, we should dwell on the analysis concerning the kind of contents that are normally found on a blog.

More precisely, we must distinguish the parts of the blog that will be updated more frequently, from the more "static" contents, which will be created in the first phase of implementation of the blog and that, thereafter, will be changed occasionally, or at least less frequently.

From this point of view, WordPress provides two elements of the blogger: **Posts** (or Articles) and **Pages**.

Posts (or, less commonly, articles) are contents that are generally organized according to a chronological order (we have already said that a blog is a kind of online diary, therefore, as such, it can not ignore that order), including texts, images and / or other multimedia contents. They are the main reason for the existence of a blog. For example, in a blog concerning games for consoles, including a typical posts will be reviews, news about new titles, and so on. In practice, will be used for every contents characterized by enormous dynamism, which vary with a clear frequency.

Pages, instead, are used for contents that does not fall into this chronological organization, because more static.

It must be emphasized that, generally, the term "page" means any document in HTML format, viewable with a browser. According to the terminology of WordPress, instead, the page consists of a particular functionality available on this CMS.

During the organization of a typical blog, we find, as pages, the classic "About Us" or, as generally present in many web sites, the "Contact Us" page. Instead, for all kinds of contents for which the chronological order assumes a certain importance, it is usual to use the posts.

A practical example of blog: mybook.space4tutorial.com

During the following pages, both of this chapter and the next, we will discover and explore the different aspects of WordPress, using implementation of our sample blog, accessible at the following link: http://mybook.space4tutorial.com.

First, we start creating pages.

In the blog that we are going to create, in particular, we will publish n. 3 pages and some example posts.

In this way, we can work creating a structure that is very similar than most of the blog available on Internet.

The following are pages that we will create:

- **About Us** - this page will contain the information about us and our blog;
- **Our Mission** - it indicate our main topics and objectives of our blog;
- **Contacts** - it will contain information to enable our readers to contact us.

Before beginning to post contents on our blogs, we must keep in mind that, regardless you want to create a new page, rather than a new post and vice versa, the tools that the WordPress CMS makes available to the blogger are substantially the same, with some exceptions which will be highlighted in the following pages.

For example, tools and features related to text formatting, upload of images and other multimedia content, creation of bulleted or numbered lists, and so on, are available both for the creation of pages and posts.

Therefore, beyond the specific aspects that characterize the pages and the posts, the other common elements will be treated only once.

Pages - my first page

After the necessary clarifications, we'll now analyze, from a practical standpoint, load of contents in our blog! And we'll do it starting from the "*pages*". In the logic of WordPress and this book, as we already said, the pages will be used for those contents that more static respect to others and that, generally, we want to be always available from every part of the blog, via a menu.

That said, let's create our first page. As written in the previous section, our intention is to create 3 pages, so let's start from the first: "About Us".

Let's access the administration panel of our blog (http://mybook.space4tutorial.com/wp-admin/ in the example we're developing) and let's click on "Pages" menu item. Inside, there is a submenu with two entries. The first is "All Pages" and allows us to see a list of all pages in the blog, while the second, "Add new", permit us to create a new page.

We must start by saying that during the installation process, a sample page and a post with a comment were already created.

Therefore, by clicking on "All pages", we will show the list of pages on the blog and we will note that there's already one, called "Sample Page".

So, let's remove this page, so we can start with a situation that is as clean as possible. To delete this page, let's follow these steps, the order:

- let's position the mouse pointer on the title "Sample page". 4 links will appear just below the title: "Edit", "Quick Edit", "Trash", "View";
- let's click on the "Trash" link.

Now, we will see our page disappear into thin air. It has not been eliminated permanently, and it still exists on the database, but it's not available to readers of our blog because it's placed in the "trash", in a similar manner as the removal of files, for majority of operating systems available on the market.

Now, we can create our first page. We decide to start from the "About Us" page.

To create a new page, we can choose to click on the link "Add new" positioned on top-left corner of the current page, or to select the specific submenu on left-side of the screen.

Regardless of our choice, opting to create a new page, we find ourselves in a screen similar to the following:

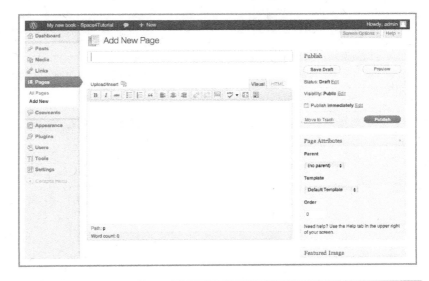

Within this screen, we can find all necessary options for the realization of our page.

More precisely, in a standard installation of WordPress, we can find:

- the text box for the page's title;
- The box concerning the content we're going to enter, with two tabs, "Visual" and "HTML", which will allow us to choose whether to write our page as if we were writing a document with a word processor (eg.: Microsoft Word, LibreOffice Writer, etc..), or lets you work with HTML tags, if you know this markup language. Unless it's necessary, we will usually work in a visual way;
- the "Publish" box, which allows us to define the state of the page, its visibility, or the start date of publication;
- the "Page Attributes" box, where you can choose, for example, ordering respect to other pages, useful when creating the menu;
- the box "Featured Image", used by many graphic templates to show a representative image of the page. This can often give a much more professional aspect to your blog.

Let us dwell on the content box. We said that it allows you to write the body of your page in Visual mode, or HTML. If we choose the default mode, precisely the "Visual", we can see several buttons, and many of them are very similar to those that can be found within a word processor (example: Word).

This visual mode is obtained by the use of a "WYSIWYG" editor (What You See Is What You Get).

By clicking on the last button to the right, we can increase the number of these buttons and we can access many other features, useful in writing a page.

If we place the mouse pointer over each one of these buttons, we can see a tooltip, an online tip which points out the features on offer.

Features offered by the various keys on the first line are the following, in order as they appear:

- Bold;
- Italic;
- Strikethrough;
- Unordered list;
- Ordered list;
- Blockquote;
- Align Left;
- Align Center;
- Align Right;
- Insert / Edit link;
- Unlink;
- Insert More Tag (primarily used in posts to create an abstract and to make the rest of the content available only to users who click on "Read more...");
- Toggle Spellchecker;
- Toggle Fullscreen mode;
- Show / Hide Kitchen Sink (extended menu);

Here, instead, are listed the functions concerning buttons on the second line:
- Paragraph style;
- Underline;
- Align full (Justify);
- Select text color;
- Paste as Plain Text;
- Paste from Word (useful for pasting other type of text, with formatting information);
- Remove formatting;
- Insert custom character;
- Outdent;
- Indent;
- Undo;
- Redo;
- Help (online help about features of all button);

Besides the features shown above, we must add that we have the ability to upload images and other multimedia content, using the "Upload / Insert" link, located above the two rows of buttons. We can use this link to create our pages or posts.

At this point you may wonder, *"Posts? But the topic of this paragraph it's not Pages?"*.

Well, yes, you read that right!

In fact, WordPress provides a toolbar identical for writing posts. And, indeed, it could not be otherwise, since content of a page is a mix of text, hyperlinks and images, the same way as posts.

Well, now we just have to create our first page "About Us".

Let's write, in the title box, the text "About Us". Instead, in the body of page, we can put anything you want, or better, what we think is useful to describe our blog.

During the writing of our first page, we decide to format certain words of text with bold and underline style. To do this, we work as we would with any word processor, namely by selecting the text with the mouse and clicking on the corresponding buttons (**B** for bold text and <u>U</u> for underline).

Furthermore, we adopt the justified style throughout the text, selecting it and pressing the corresponding button (the third on the second row of toolbar) in order to give our page a more professional look and make the text easier to read.

Finally, we insert an unordered list and a hyperlink to http://www.space4tutorial.com, the main blog of the domain space4tutorial.com.

With regard to hyperlink, clicking on the "Insert / Edit link" button (the one with the chain intact, not broken), we can see a dialog window of WordPress, where we can enter the details of the link:

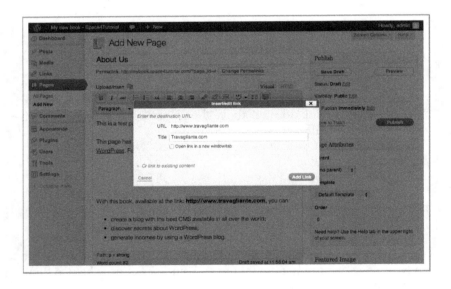

Having done this, simply click on the button "Add link" and go on.

At this stage, my personal suggestion is to try functionality of all buttons available in this screen, to learn their behavior and appearance that can give contents of the blog.

At the end of our work, the page will look as follows:

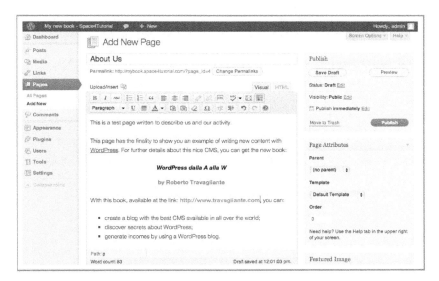

We are one step closer to create our first page. At any time, we can save the state of our work by clicking on the "Save Draft" button.

This button is useful because we can save a draft version of our page, without posting and making it available to our readers.

Moreover, in the same frame, there are 2 buttons, "Preview" and "Publish". The first allows us to check how our page appears to users of the blog, while the second allows us to publish our work.

Still, we can define the kind of "visibility" that we want to give to our page, that is, if we want to make its content accessible to all users, only those who have signed up and accessed to WordPress, or only those who know the password which was defined when creating the page, by author.

The last two options can be useful especially in the case of a blog of "collaborative" kind, managed by different people.

We can also set a publish date and time. But we will discuss this feature in paragraph titled "Posts - My first post", below on this chapter, because it is most useful for posts, when we wish to program their publication.

That said, let's click on "Publish" button. In this way, the page will be published on the blog and it will be accessible to everyone in the world.

We can now test it out, visiting our blog. More precisely, we will find the main menu item "About Us", which will allow us to display the page we just created.

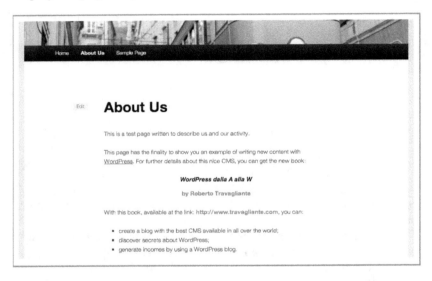

Obviously, from the graphical point of view, our blog still looks very simple. Later we will see how to change effectively the graphics through the use of themes (or templates).

Let's create the other two pages

Using the information and knowledge gained in the previous chapter, let's create the other two pages. Still select the menu "Pages" → "Add new".

Let's create a new page with the following information:

Title:
Our Mission
Content:
This is a new page, in which denote our motivations and objectives we intend to pursue with this blog.
Obviously, this is a test text, you can put anything you want, on your blog.

Finally, let's click on "Publish" button. Again, we must create the "Contacts" page, so we again select menu "Pages" → "Add new" and we prepare a page with the following data:

Title:
Contacts
Content:
This page contains references for contacting me.
More precisely, to contact the author of this blog, you can use the following email address:
book [at] space4tutorial [dot] com
or:
info [at] space4tutorial [dot] com

If, like me, you hate email SPAM (unsolicited advertising) and you hate when you find dozens of mails per day in your mailbox, then I must open a small parenthesis: why we indicate an email address with "[at]" and "[dot]," rather than with the "@" and ".""?

This is a precaution to make sure that this address can not be detected by some software for the automated retrieval of email addresses from web sites.

In fact, our blog will be on the Internet and, therefore, it will be potentially accessible by users from all over the world.

And, as on the Internet there are also automated software used by SPAM companies, specialized in sending SPAM and able to scan the Web for email addresses to which they can send commercial email of any kind, you may wish to show your addresses in a special format, so that their recognition is made more difficult.

Often, these software try sequences of characters in the following form: <<u>aaaaa@bbbbbbb.ccc</u>> (generally corresponding to e-mail addresses) and / or "mailto:" links.

When they find an email address, they store it in special databases.

Then, collected email addresses are sent to "spambots", robots that take care of sending spam emails, without any prior authorization (as required by "CAN-SPAM Act of 2003", made law by U.S. President George W. Bush and now considered a common reference at international level, for all those activities related to email marketing), concerning the purchase of products, adhesion to special services, and so on.

So, when you publish an email address on a blog, you should always use the alternate characters for "disturbing" the detection from potential "non-human" visitors (typically software named "bots").

Anyway, coming back to the drafting of our pages, once we have uploaded content, we can click again on "Publish" button, to get our page online.

If we did everything correctly, we should find two new pages, as clearly visible within the administrative panel:

Good! Now we're ready to write our first article, or to use the typical terminology of a blog, our first post.

Posts - my first post

After viewing how to create a page, we can consider writing an article a task of extreme simplicity.

In fact, there is not much difference, especially if we consider that writing posts is made through the use of a "Visual" editor very similar to that employed for the preparation of the pages.

So in this section we will focus primarily on the elements that characterize the creation of an article / post, compared to a page.

Immediately start: what the menu should be used? You can guess it? Well, surely "Posts"!

As for pages, there is a default post, titled "Hello world". We can decide whether or not to delete this post and, in the first case, the steps to follow are very similar to those related to the deletion of a page, discussed in the previous paragraph.

What we are interested now, however, is the creation of a new post, so let's click on the submenu "Add New", available in the menu "Posts".

The screen that appears is very similar to the following:

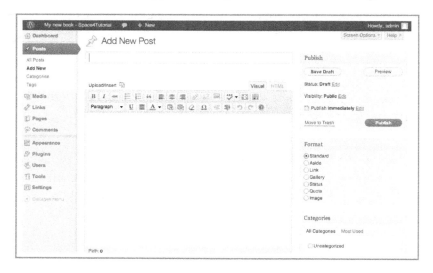

We immediately note a screen which is very similar to that relating to the creation of a new page. However, on the right side, there are several panels which are not present in the creation of a page.

In particular, apart from the section "Format", which we will make a brief mention in a moment, the most important parts are those related to management of Categories and Tags.

In fact, in a blog the management of these two elements is very important and, often, is crucial from the point of view of SEO (Search Engine Optimization).

However, for now, it suffices to know that through these frames you can add new categories and tags, in relation to the contents loaded on the blog.

That said, let's create a post, just now, containing some formatted text, the way you prefer. In the case of the blog mybook.space4tutorial.com, we will create more than one post, with sample text.

As we did when we created our first page, let's fill the form, with the title *"Test Post no. 1"* and the content *"This is the content of the post n. 1. In this post has been added plain text, only to give you an example of post"*.

Theoretically, once entered title and content of the post, we are ready to publish it. However, we prefer to do more.

We want to create a category where we can place all these posts we will create. So, let's move to the square "Categories".

Let's click on the link "*+ Add New Category*" and, in the text box that appears, let's write "*News*". Finally, let's click on the button "*Add a new category*". Now, we will notice a new category "*News*" is selected. Our post is ready to be inserted within this new category.

At this point, we may determine start date and start time of post publishing, using the appropriate entry in box "*Publish*". This feature is sometimes overlooked by bloggers, but we may want to schedule a different date, from which the post may be viewed by users of the blog.

For example, it may be useful for bloggers who want to ensure the continued publication of at least one new post per day, but can not write posts every day, because he is busy for other works during the week.

Through this option, he may decide to write at least 7 posts during every weekend, scheduling the publication of a post per day, from Monday until the following week.

Personally, I think that is pretty hard to constantly update a blog, giving the rate of one post per day. Instead, using the programming feature of posts, the content management of the blog is much easier.

However, regardless of the date of publication set, let's click on the "Publish" button and go and see our new post, selecting the home page of our blog.

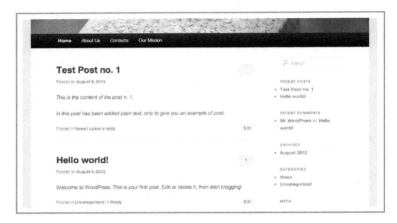

Media management

An important issue, both in the case of creating a page and a new post, is management of pictures.

In fact, our blog, at the moment, in addition to default image provided by the standard theme for WordPress, has no media contents.

Therefore, it may seem somewhat "ugly". So, we absolutely must do something to improve its appearance. Later in this book we will see how to change the layout of the blog, but for now we begin and improve the posts and pages created by inserting some images.

For example, in the page *"About Us"*, we can use an image to better represent our blog. In case of Space 4 Tutorial, we insert image of a book, that we previous downloaded from the Internet. With the image located in a designated folder on our local computer, let's click on the menu "Posts" → "All Posts" and, finally, on the title of post where we wish to add the image.

In this way, we can reach the screen concerning Post modification.

In the body of the post, let's choose the point in the text where we want to show this image, placing the cursor at that point. Finally, let's click on "Upload / Insert".

A window will appear similar to the following:

At this point we can choose to use the *"drag & drop"* to upload the image on our web space, or alternatively we can click on the "Select File" button, which will open a dialog box for selecting the image file.

In any case, once completed upload of the image, the screen that appears will be very similar to the following:

Thanks to this screen, we can define different aspects of the images and the way they should appear with the text, for example whether they should be left-aligned or right-aligned, if they must be accompanied by a caption, if they must be "linkable" and lead to specific page, etc...

After defining the different options, let's click on the "Insert into Post". Now, we can see the image into the post and / or the page that we are updating.

To confirm these changes, we must click on the "Update" button, which has replaced the "Publish" button. This, because the post (or page) has been previously published.

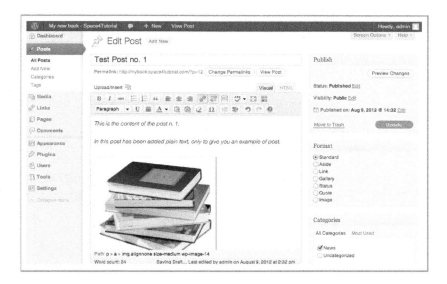

At this stage, we can view our post on the blog and, where appropriate, we can determine whether we need to make further updates to it.

Often, when editing an article, can be useful to use the button "Preview Changes", which allows us to have a constant visual feedback of the work we are doing and, if necessary, to correct any formatting problems that may occur.

Other available options for pages and posts

There are other options and useful features for creating pages and posts, in addition to those shown above. Below, we report some of them:

- **Featured Image:** it allows you to link an image to a post and / or a page, which can be used as a thumbnail in order to characterize the post and / or the page itself. This feature is related to the use of a graphic theme that allows the use of the featured images.

- **Move to Trash:** it allows you to delete the post and / or the page. In the default configuration of Wordpress, the deletion makes use of a trash that can retrieve the contents removed, if you need.
- **Order:** this option affects only pages (posts follow chronological order). You can order any page, by assigning it a number.
- **Format:** this option affects only posts. It allows you to determine how they should be treated and showed by the current theme.

As they are very intuitive options, we only indicate their mean. Moreover, they are not essential to get started with a blog and they usage can be further investigated later.

Chapter 6 - Improving blog structure

Quick editing of pages and posts

After analyzing how to create a page and a post with WordPress, let's see how we can change some aspects, quickly, through the feature named "Quick Edit".

It is a possibility that is offered by WordPress, and we use it when we need to change some elements for a page and / or a post, such as title, publish start-date, the type of access (with password and / or private), categories, tags, the ability to receive comments, status (whether draft or published), and more on...

It should be pointed out that this feature doesn't allow you to change body part of post and / or page. This means that, when you need to modify body, you must use the normal "Edit" function.

After these clarifications, let's try to use the "Quick Edit" feature to add some tags to the post that we just added to blog. Tags' names are not important, we are just interested in seeing how we can complete modifications, so we can use any names. In the example illustrated in this book, we will choose three tags: "posts", "news", and "curiosities".

By clicking on the menu "Posts" → "All Posts", we can access a list of all posts included. At the time, in our sample blog, we can find the test post n. 1 and the default post, installed during the initial configuration of WordPress.

By placing the mouse pointer over the title of one post, we can see several links and, precisely:

- Edit
- Quick Edit
- Trash
- View

Let's click on "Quick Edit". We will see a box like the following, where we will edit the options related to our post:

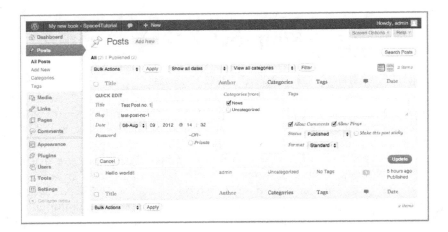

In the text-area "Tags", we must insert our 3 tags, separated by commas and click on the "Update" button.

At this stage, the "Tags" box will disappear and, under the Tags column, on the same line of newly modified post, our tags appear.

The feature "Trash"

Near the "Quick Edit" option, a special link is available for the deletion of the post and / or page.

This is the "Trash" feature, which allows to move the post (or page) within a virtual trash, in a very similar way to what happens for the deletion of files in the context of the most widely used operating systems (Windows, Linux and / or Mac OS).

In practice, posts (or pages) are not permanently removed, but simply moved between those "trash".

What does it means?

Well, that you can, at any time, restore deleted post / pages.

Let's test function, trashing the post "Hello world!". After trashed, we can see a "Trash" link on the top of post list, next to the links "All" and "Published":

If we click on it, we can see our deleted post.

And, by placing the mouse pointer over title link, we will see two entries: "Restore" and "Delete Permanently":

If we click on "Delete Permanently", then the item will be permanently removed from the database.

Instead, with the "Restore" button, we can recovery the post, which will be newly published. For the moment, since this post has also a comment that will make us comfortable during the next few pages, let's click on this link and let's restore our post.

Categories

In a blog, the use of the right categories is of fundamental importance, since it allows us to group several post of the same type, obtaining a very organized blog, in terms of contents.

For example, a food blog, where several recipes are listed, you can divide the posts into the following categories: "appetizers", "pasta", "desserts" and so on...

Again, in a blog about cars and motors, it is possible to use a more structured schema, possibly hierarchical, based on several levels, where the first level concerns car producers, and the second includes single models of cars. So, a post about the test drive of X car (belonging to Y producer), can be inserted into the Y category, and X subcategory.

Or, in the case of complex and / or multi-thematic blogs, we can use more complex structures, where categories are connected by hierarchical relationships and also in a transversal way, by branches that link them.

One category generally contains more posts and, at the same time, a post can belong to several categories, in relation to specific needs.

The choice of an appropriate category structure, in relation to the contents of the blog, allows readers to orient themselves among the different pages and, in general, it is very appreciated by new visitors. In fact, they can get a better "experience" and, therefore, enjoy our work and return on the blog in the future.

Furthermore, we must say that regardless of the kind of selected structure, categories have a key role from the perspective of SEO activities (Search Engine Optimization), as well as having the duty to "maintain order" among the various post of our blog. One of the benefits that a blog can gain from effective organization of its categories is the fact of conquering the best positions on search engine results, for certain keywords.

So, when designing the structure of your blog, I highly recommend using categories. But, of course, I suggest avoiding their use exaggerated. Personally, over time, I have seen blogs that have more categories than posts, and surely this is not the right way to creating a successful blog.

Tags

Tags are another important element of WordPress. They are labels which can be useful to connect more posts between them, based on specific keywords.

Tags also play a very important role in terms of SEO, perhaps even more than the categories, because there are not hierarchical links among them and, if they are used in a good way, they allow an improvement from the point of view of internal links, with good consequences about indexing by search engines.

Moreover, a good use of tags can result in a better navigation by visitors of our blog and greater average visit duration on our pages.

Tag or Category? This is the problem!

Many bloggers are engaged with this kind of choice. Some bloggers use exclusively categories, while others do the opposite, using only the tags and ignoring the possibility of organizing categories for their blog.

My suggestion is the following: use both and trying to do it right!

In particular, I usually employ categories to create semi-rigid groups of posts, or to define the different kinds of posts that may exist into the blog. Instead, I define tags, for each individual post, thinking about the keywords I wish to "push", those that I want to better promote because more representative of the covered topics.

For example, in a blog about computer science, the better categories could be the following:

- News
- Reviews
- Windows
- Linux
- Mac OS

while tags for a single post about a new released distribution of GNU / Linux could be the following: linux, gnu, software distribution, operating system, open sources, new releases, and so on...

However, it should be emphasized that the decisions concerning category and tag organization are very personal. So, they can be very different between a blogger and other.

For this reason, I suggest you start with a structure of categories and tags, experimenting and modifying it during construction, in relation to needs as they emerge, because this is the only way you can take a decision about the best categories and the most appropriate tags for your posts.

Chapter 7 - User participation

Comments

Creating a blog is, of course, an activity that has a certain charm, both for the expert blogger and a newbie.

However, one of the most exciting aspects of a blog is probably the ability to get an adequate interaction between the webmaster and its users.

As we mentioned in first chapter of this book, talking about "traditional" websites and forums, a blog can give us advantages of both, without inheriting their respective critical elements.

Among these positive aspects there is precisely the simplicity on managing it and the capability to involve the visitors of the blog.

In fact, users can express their opinions on covered topics and their judgments about the several posts, starting discussions which can involve many persons, especially for large blogs.

The tool with which it is possible to involve readers of your blog is the "comment system".

The "comments" are interventions performed by users on a given content, information and / or news that exists into a blog. In particular, writing a comment at a blog article, the reader has the opportunity to express his opinion and to see his intervention published together with the post, on a section of the page reserved to comments.

Probably, the comment system is one of the most important elements of a blog and if it's managed properly, it can can make the difference between a blog and a great blog.

In fact, from the point of view of the success, comments allow us:

- to obtain and retain our users;
- to allow and learn both tastes and opinions in relation to covered topics
- to understand the "target" of people who follow the site, and the expectations of everyone on particular topics

- to understand which posts are most popular, to be promoted more to get a successful blog.

Moreover, comments give a sort of "charge" to bloggers, especially for personal blogs, where they can get good feedback about written posts.

Moderation of comments

Depending on how established by the owner of the blog, comments can be immediately published or alternatively subjected to a preliminary approval, called "moderation". In the first case, comments on blogs are "free", and users can immediately see them on the blog.

Using moderation, the blogger has the opportunity to check in advance if comments written by users can be published, and he can decide to approve or remove them, based on what are the preferences of those who administer, in terms of editorial and contents, the blog.

Moderation can be useful for the most different reasons. These reasons vary according to the preferences of the blogger.

In fact, under some circumstances, the blogger decides to turn on moderation to prevent users from posting offensive / sexual / SPAM comments on the blog.

In particular, this kind of comment is often considered a problem, more and more felt as the blog grows.

It's important to point out that different platforms for creating blogs, including Wordpress, allow us to include links to web sites along with comments. So, many people fill the blogosphere with "fake comments" in order to promote one or more websites, concerning topics that don't have nothing to do with our blog.

Often, especially after a week since the beginning of our blogging activity, we can start getting comments from unknown users, containing generic phrases, that are not related to posts where they are inserted, such as: "Well done, good post!", "Your post is very interesting!","Nice blog, I will add it to my bookmarks!", and so on.

These comments, although apparently written by people interested in the blog, sometimes show links to websites of dubious morality, or hyperlinks left by some users to get visits on websites related to services and / or products of any kind.

However, as discussed later, in addition to using the instrument of "moderation", in order to eliminate this type of comments we can use some WordPress plugins for automated removal of spam comments.

We can also configure WordPress to use moderation for only certain types of comments, leaving all "free". In following pages, we will learn in practice what are the different options available on WordPress to manage moderation of comments.

How do we write comments on a blog?

We are going to see it now, accessing to the homepage of our blog. From there, we move to the post which we created earlier, in our case "Test Post no. 1".

We will notice that immediately below the content of the post there is a section dedicated to comments, with an invitation to comment such as "Leave a comment" or "Leave a reply".

If we have already logged into the admin panel of the blog, this section will appear as showed in the screenshot above, with a statement such as "Logged in as admin. Log out?".

In practice, WordPress recognizes us as users and doesn't ask further information for identification. It only asks to write a comment.

Clicking on "Log out?", We can disconnect us from WordPress, and be seen as normal people, not authenticated.

Under these conditions, the same section will appear in this other way:

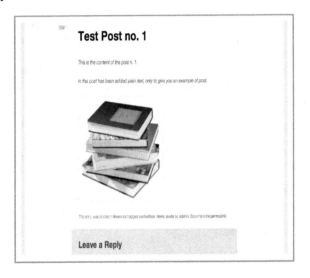

In practice, WordPress asks us to enter a name, an email address and possibly a link to our website.

As we will see the following pages, we can modify the behavior of WordPress relative to the comments, through the admin panel, but in its default configuration the name and email address are required fields.

Let's test: let's write a comment to the post, filling all the fields and clicking on submit button, located on the same page in bottom of the screen.

In the default configuration comments go into moderation queue, so our comment will not be made available until an administrator (that's us) will moderate it. In this case, WordPress will report us that "The comment is awaiting moderation":

So, let's moderate newly written comment by logging into admin panel.

From the administration panel of WordPress, we can view comments in moderation queue using the menu "Comments".

In addition, through the dashboard we can obtain some information, within the "Current Status" section, as the total number of comments, the number of approved comments, comments to moderate and comments recognized as spam.

As we noted in the chapter concerning creation of pages and posts, during the initial configuration of the blog a sample comment is automatically installed. If we didn't remove the sample post, or if we restored it as described in Chapter 6, this comment should appear in the "Comments" page, along with the new comment that we just inserted:

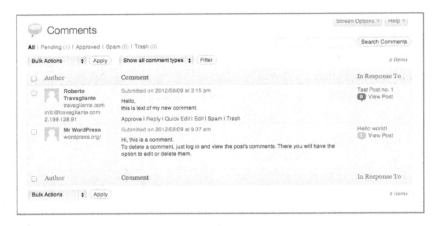

As we can see in the screenshot above, just under the heading "Comments", we can find several links that allow us to display the comments, classified in:
- already approved comments;
- pending comments (awaiting moderation);
- comments detected as spam;
- removed comments (or better, trashed).

For every comment we can see various information, including the name entered by the person who left it on our blog, possibly a link to his site, date and time, the post which it refers to, and email address.

In addition, comments in moderation queue are showed with a yellow color for background and, if we place the mouse pointer over one of them, we can see some links that allow us to intervene on the comment in various ways.

To approve the comment, we must click on "Approve". Other features include:
- the capability to respond to comments directly from the administration panel;
- the ability to edit and quick edit comment;
- the capability to report the comment as spam;
- finally, the capability to trash the comment.

Once the comment is approved, the yellow background is replaced with a white background. At this point, the comment is published and it's visible to everyone. Anytime you can go back, click on "Unapprove" which replaces the "Approve" link when the comment is no longer in moderation queue.

Censorship? No, thank you!

Comment moderation is a very important aspect of maintaining a blog, and it requires special attention. But at the same time it must never become useless censure.

In fact, I believe that one of the most exciting aspects of a blog is that a blog provides a "virtual window" to the web, related to people's behavior and their way to act towards others, about specific topics and / or problems.

The "social" feature of a blog has as a consequence that people are encouraged to express themselves, in a way similar to discussions within a group of friends.

This often leads users to take net positions on certain issues, which don't necessarily coincide with our.

Under these circumstances, the main temptation for many bloggers is to use moderation to censor comments of users with whom we don't agree, removing them with no reason.

During my blogging activity, especially in the beginning, I often asked myself things like, "What I have to do with this comment? I have to delete it? Or I have to publish it, whether if I don't agree with this comment?".

Well, I want to say right now that my conclusion is that censorship is not a good way to blog.

First, censorship does not help us to change what our users think. Also, it prevents the blog to receive good contribution from people who, perhaps, have some good reason to write specific comments.

The use of comment moderation as a "tool for censorship" is only useful to gradually exclude people from the blog. In fact, if our users see that their comments are not published, then they move away, or worse, they start and send negative (and sometimes offensive) comments about our conduct, both on our blog and on other similar websites. And this can be a big problem for our reputation!

We know that user's participation for the blog is an element that makes the difference between a normal blogs and a successful blog. And, if we want to encourage participation in our blog, we have to welcome our readers, as they are at home, that is free to express themselves. Of course, if they respect other users.

This means that if someone moves constructive criticism about our posts, then we must give him the right space, trying to understand his motives. And if we disagree, then we can talk in a civilized and peaceful, exposing our arguments.

In fact, if they are valid, then we can even persuade our counterparts and gain new loyal users.

Furthermore, we can give space to other people, to intervene enriching the discussion.

So, our blog will earn fame and will become a good place for discussion, where comment activity is nice and worthwhile.

For all the reasons stated above, after spending 5 years following the magical world of blogging, I think the best solution to achieve a successful blog is to leave all the comments free, except for those that have at least one or two links in the text, or that contain swear words and other offensive language.

The latter type of comments can be filtered using the special feature concerning the comment's blacklist, which will be discussed in the next paragraph.

Settings for comments

Regard to management of comments, WordPress has several options concerning the various elements of the blog, that can be reached via the menu "Settings" → "Discussion".

In particular, using these settings, you can define all the methods of interaction from every users of our blog.

For example, through this screen we can allow to comment only to persons who registered to our blog as users, preventing occasional visitors to write their comments.

Or alternatively, we can establish that the comment author must fill his name and his email address (as required fields).

Or, we can decide that every time someone writes a comment, the administrator must receive a notification via email. We can also enable or disable moderation of comments, or we can restrict it to only those comments containing a certain number of links (A common characteristic of comment spam is a large number of hyperlinks).

An interesting peculiarity is that we can establish the words for which comments must be considered spam, or must be placed in moderation queue.

This feature can be very useful, for example to prevent users from writing swear words or other bad expressions within comments.

In particular, for this purpose WordPress provides two text areas. In it we can write different keywords (or expressions formed by several words), one for each row. So, these keywords can be used to discriminate comments to be considered SPAM or to put into the moderation queue.

Using this page you can also configure chronological order for comments, establishing which of them have to be showed first (older or newer comments), at the top of each page.

In addition, we can define many options and, based on our choices, we can make our blog more or less participative, from the point of view of users.

Pingbacks

In addition to the comments in the strict sense, WordPress is able to handle a very particular kind of comment: the Pingback.

Pingbacks, really, are not real comments, even if they are shown in the same window of the latter. More precisely, the pingback system should be considered as a protocol useful to receive notifications from other websites. Every notification is received when another website inserts a link directed to our blog.

In practice, WordPress treats a pingback as a comment and, when another website places a direct link to a post from our blog, our blog receives this type of comment, and it normally displays it along with the other comments in the post.

Pingbacks are very useful, because they indicate us when other bloggers mentioning our blog into their posts. Moreover, they help us understand whether our blog is considered by others a high quality blog. In fact, except in situations where someone mentions us expressing a negative opinion, if someone decides to insert a link to our blog, then we can usually get an indication that the contents within it are worthy of interest.

Chapter 8 - Look and feel of the blog

The importance of layout

In previous chapters, we learnt the most important elements related to inclusion of web contents (pages and / or posts) into a blog.

In addition, we saw how we can manage the comments received on the blog and how we can encourage the participation of our users.

But a blog is not content only. Obviously, pages and posts are the backbone of a blog, so if there are low-quality contents, users will decide to go away and it will be difficult to newly attract them.

However, one element that drives visitors to enjoy a blog from the beginning is, of course, its look and feel.

In fact, a blog with an eye-catching graphics attracts the user much more than a blog where the look and feel was not adequately treated.

As already mentioned in Chapter 3, there is ample evidence that, on average, a user measures an interesting site in a very limited time interval, usually within about 5 seconds.

Obviously, in 5 seconds he has no way to evaluate the contents, that is the text within posts. It would be unthinkable to be able to read a web page, maybe full of text, in just five seconds.

Therefore, it is clear that the only factors that affect, even at an unconscious level, the decision to stay on website or, alternatively, to leave it, are the graphics and, at most, the words of the text put in some evidence (for example, the words in bold or underlined).

Hence the need to create a website that is graphically attractive, not necessarily, as I sometimes say, "a spacial blog", but a blog that is structured in order to be pleasant and easy to read. This is because if the initial impact is positive and it is attracting attention at a subconscious level, then the user will focus in reading the textual contents.

On the contrary, if the impact is negative, then the user will run away in less than a second!

To test effects that the graphics can produce on ourselves when we visit a website, let's look at the following two screenshots.

The first screenshot concerns the blog that we are creating during the writing of these pages (http://mybook.space4tutorial.com):

The second screenshot belongs to the main blog of Space 4 Tutorial (http://www.space4tutorial.com), and is obtained by using a freely available WordPress theme.

I have not directly developed this theme, but I just found it on repository available on wordpress.org. It was installed on the blog by following a simple procedure that we will see in the following pages:

Now, let us ask: Which of these websites raises a greater curiosity? Although tastes in terms of graphics are very personal and can vary greatly from one person to another, I believe that most of visitors may prefer a website with a layout closer to the second screenshots, rather than the first.

As a visitor, I think that I'm willing to dwell more on the main blog of Space 4 Tutorial, rather than on the blog http://mybook.space4tutorial.com.

On the Internet we can find many examples of websites that made their fortunes thanks to an appealing graphic structure, as well as many examples of corporate sites that, with an inadequate graphic layout, did not achieve success.

For this reason, in the following paragraphs we will see how WordPress allows us to work on the appearance of the blog and, more specifically, how we can make our attractive blog, in a few clicks and using only tools provided by this great CMS.

WordPress themes

The layout of a blog based on WordPress is managed by the so-called "themes" or "templates".

A WordPress theme consists of several .PHP files, which interact one with each other to provide the graphical interface of the blog, using a set of functions provided by WordPress itself, for displaying different blog's elements.

More precisely, WordPress provides several functions that may be useful if we want to have a more complete control of all the features of the blog. These functions are used for different purposes and they are executed by specific calls located within .PHP files of graphic themes.

For example, by using these functions, a theme is able to show the content of a post and / or a page (function "the_content()"), or it can show the list of categories (function "wp_list_categories()"), or comments related to a specific post ("wp_list_comments()"), and so on...

In this book we are not going to study details of these functions, because we don't need this to get a professional and aesthetically pleasing blog.

Moreover, this book is intended for everyone, even those who are unfamiliar with the language PHP.

However, if you wish to learn more about these topics, just know that every WordPress theme makes extensive use of these functions and more details are available on the Internet, mainly on the WordPress Codex website (http://codex.wordpress.org/), that is the official online manual of WordPress the best official source of information for the developer who wants to create themes and plugins for this great platform.

That said, we can handle graphics in WordPress, by using the "Appearance" menu, located into the administrative panel of the blog.

The "Appearance" menu allows, in effect, to virtually perform all activities relating to the graphical layout of the blog, starting from installation and activation of a specific theme, to management of the lateral bar (sidebar) and the menu, up to the editing of individual files that make up the theme.

That said, let's begin and change the look and feel of our blog, by installing a new theme. There are two ways to install a WordPress theme.

The first one consists in copying the folder containing all the files that make up the theme, into the directory "wp-content/themes/" located in our web space, in the main directory of blog. This option is possible in all cases where we have the ability to upload files on the web space dedicated to our blog.

This way is not practicable under specific conditions, for example when our blog is created by using the free platform wordpress.com, which however provides many themes characterized by a certain level of customization.

An infinite number of free and commercial themes is available on the Internet. To install one of them, just follow these steps:

- Search the theme on the Internet, through search engines;
- Download the theme from the website of its creator (if the theme is licensed for commercial use, you have to complete payment transaction for it). Generally, the theme will be available as an archive. So, unpack .ZIP;
- Unzip the .ZIP file into a folder;
- Read, if exists, the README or INSTALL file for more information on installation process and features of the theme;
- Upload the folder containing theme's files on the web space, precisely into the directory "wp-content/themes/".

About this last point, the upload can be done via a FTP client software as CyberDuck, already described in Chapter 4, when we performed the first installation of WordPress.

We must pay attention to the fact that different themes are provided with some support files, such as images used on it (in vector format). These files should not be loaded on the web space, but simply used by the blogger to change some elements of the theme, customizing it to suit his needs. In these cases, only folder containing the theme's files should be uploaded into the "themes", excluding others. For more information, we may usually refer to instructions that are provided by the respective developers of the choosen themes.

In addition to this way, WordPress makes available to the bloggers a faster and simpler method to install a theme. It consists in using a special feature made available through the administration panel.

Unlike the previous method, this one is not always practicable, especially for themes provided with commercial license, which are often sent as .ZIP archives to our e-mail, after a payment process.

In addition, this option is not practicable in all the cases where the theme is not made available by its creator through the official repository of WordPress themes (http://wordpress.org/extend/themes/) that we will see in the following pages.

To install a theme with this method, let's access the administration panel of the blog, menu "Appearance" → "Themes".

The following screen shows all the currently installed themes, as well as the currently activated one.

We can activate one of the available themes by clicking on specific link located under its preview image ("Activate"). It's important to note that, especially in the early phases of creation of our blog, we can also install more themes and choose the best among them, activating it at a second time.

To install a new theme, we can use the "Appearance" menu and select the tab "Install Themes". Within this tab, we can look for the type of theme that we want, by using various criteria as, for example, a keyword, or a predominant color, or the number of columns, or the layout type (fixed or variable-width), or the presence of special features (as CSS tools, featured images, nested comments), etc..

Let's try this: let's look for a theme with 2 columns, with only one sidebar, whose main color is green. In practice, let's select the relevant options and let's click on the "Find Themes" button located at the bottom of the page.

The result will consist of one or more pages containing a number of themes with the required characteristics:

For each of these themes, a screenshot is shown, with a brief description and three hyperlinks:

- **Install Now**: it allows us to directly install the theme;
- **Preview**: it allows us to view a demo of the theme;
- **Details**: it displays additional information such as the version number of the theme, the author's name and evaluation received by users, from 1 to 5 stars.

Let's try to install a theme, among the ones that we obtained by search and that were shown on this page. Let's choose what we like best and then just click "Install now". This will open a confirmation box, where we will click "Install" button.

At this point, the theme chosen will be downloaded and installed on our blog. However, to view results of our operations, we need to activate it. So, we must return to the page accessible from the menu "Appearance" → "Themes".

After installation, the theme will be visible within those available and it can be activated by clicking on "Activate" button.

Here is the blog http://mybook.space4tutorial.com, after activating a new theme:

Uh! What's happened? Don't worry, we have just enabled our new theme. And our blog has completely changed appearance, in a few clicks!

There is still much to do to improve appearance of this blog, but now we know how to change completely its look and feel, at any time and with a few clicks.

Widgets

When choosing the theme for our blog, we must pay attention to the support of some features that can represent elements of great simplification with regard to the graphical structure of the blog.

In particular, themes available for WordPress may or may not support Widgets.

Widgets are an important tool for customizing the graphical layout of the blog. The most common function of the widget is to simplify life to bloggers, about the arrangement of the different elements within the sidebar (or sidebars, if more than one).

For some time WordPress allows management of widgets, but not all themes (especially those developed not just recently) will support this feature.

If we decide to use a theme that doesn't support widgets, and we do need to intervene, for example, on a sidebar, we will be forced to change the code of some .PHP pages of the theme. This can become the only way to include any element (as, for example, a search box, the list of categories, etc.).

Instead, thanks to system of "widgets", the same operation can be handled easily by using mouse, in less than 10 seconds.

Moreover, moving from one theme to another, settings concerning widgets do not change. For example, if we actived a Calendar, among other widgets, on a theme called "Theme X", then when we decide to install and activate a new "Theme Y", we shall find this widget in the sidebar, graphically modified consistently with the style of the new theme.

Therefore, we strongly suggest choosing a theme that supports widgets.

To manage the widgets of our blog, we choose the menu "Appearance" → "Widgets".

In page of WordPress concerning widgets, we can find the available widgets in the left side, while on right side we can see the boxes corresponding to different areas where they can be placed.

In our case, we can see an area on the right side that corresponds to the sidebar shown on all pages of the blog, along with an area that refers to sidebar displayed when you go to a WordPress page (intended as specific element of WordPress as "About Us" page).

To activate one of the widget, simply drag the respective item, with the mouse, inside one of the boxes located on the left.

Moreover, for each widget is possible to determine certain characteristics.

In our case, for example, we have decided that in the sidebar should be shown the search form, the 5 most recent articles, the 5 most recent comments, the widget "archives", the list of categories and the widget "meta" (which contains specific links to go to the administrative panel of the blog with a click).

To establish, in detail, the characteristics of individual widgets activated on our blog, we need to click on the arrow pointing downwards and located on the right of each of them. For example, for the "Recent Comments" widget, you can define the number of comments to display on screen:

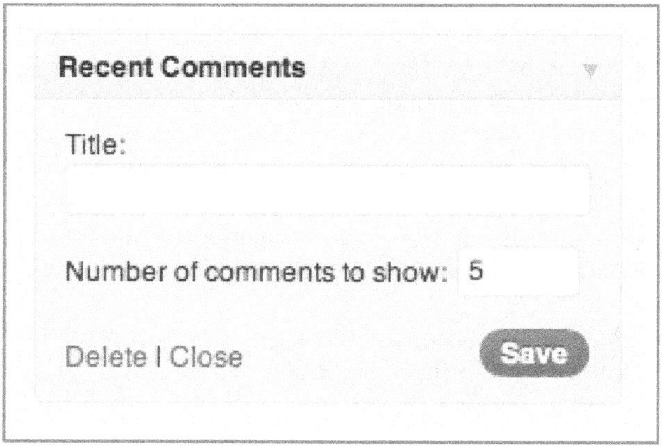

Recent Comments ▼

Title:

Number of comments to show: 5

Delete | Close   **Save**

In the default view, under the available widgets, we also find a frame concerning deactivated widgets. This frame may be used in case we decide to stop using a widget, but we don't want to lose its characteristics.

Let's think, for example, about the "Text" widget, which allows us to enclose arbitrary text or HTML code to our website.

Using the box concerning not active widgets, we can disable this widget without losing its text or HTML content.

In this way, if we later want to re-insert the widget in the sidebar, we do not need to rewrite the text / HTML code inside it.

Menus

Menus are another theme's feature that should not be underestimated. Of course, even a theme that does not support menus can display them on the blog. But WordPress offers a very simplified management for menu and if you experience it, you can't live without.

Menus are configurable via the menu item "Layout" → "Menu".

This section of the WordPress administration panel allows, by a manner very similar to the widget manager, menu creation for our blog.

In it we can find several boxes, but we can consider them as divided into two main parts. The left side contains the box where you define the menu arrangement within the theme (a theme can be configured to have more than a menu). In addition, it contains the types of menu items that can be used. The right side, instead, contains menus grouped by a classification represented with several tabs.

In our example, we will create a menu with two entries. The first will be our home page, while the second will be represented by the "About Us" page.

To add a new menu, on the right side, let's click on the tab with the symbol "+" and then let's click "Save Menu".

Next, let's define the position for our menu, by selecting it via the dropdown list box in the "Theme Location" and, then, by clicking "Save" button.

Finally, let's select, from the "Pages" box, "Show All" tab, the menu items we want, by clicking on "Add to menu" button. At this point, the screen should appear roughly as the following:

Let's click on "Save Menu" and we're done!

If we look at the blog, we will see the new menu, as modified by us, at the top left (we have also chosen a new theme):

Now, performing the same procedure given above, we can also add the menu items concerning the pages titled "Our Mission" and "Contact us".

The theme options, the background and the header

In addition to support for widgets and menus, the theme that we have installed may also support other specific options, which can be defined in a section made available by the developer who created the theme itself.

When a theme has custom options, into the menu "Appearance" may be shown a submenu dedicated to these options that, for example, can allow us to change background colors and text, to show some additional elements (for example, a slideshow which rotates featured images belonging to posts of the blog), or buttons for social bookmarking (buttons for sharing on facebook, twitter, etc...).

These options can also allow us the insertion of scripts related to advertising channels on our blog.

Using these options may allow the blogger to get a high customization level of our blog, making it almost "unique", even compared to other blogs that use the same theme.

In addition to specific options of installed theme, via the administrative panel of the blog, and specifically the "Appearance" menu, we can handle two important elements: the background and the header of the blog.

In particular, through two submenus "Background" and "Header", we can upload images for use as header and background. All this, without writing a single line of HTML or PHP.

However, if you wish to have total control over blog's layout, without any kind of restriction and without knowing PHP and HTML, you can always resort to the editor made available by WordPress.

PHP editor

Themes of WordPress are composed of different files that interact with each other. This makes themes very modular, so we can potentially modify any part of them in a simple way. For example, if we know just a bit of PHP language, we can intervene on a theme and modify header, sidebar and more possible, according to our needs, through the specific files (for example header.php, sidebar.php, etc.).

This makes life easier for bloggers, but also to persons those who want to edit a theme from an existing one, to customize their own blogs.

For this activity, WordPress provides a built-in editor for theme's files, which is reachable via the menu "Appearance" → "Editor".

By using this editor, we can modify individual components of the active theme or other themes that are currently installed but not activated, selecting the relevant files through the links shown on the right of the screen:

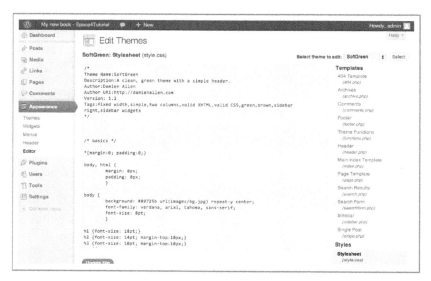

Usually, in most WordPress themes there are the following files:

- **index.php**: it shows the main page of blog (homepage);
- **page.php**: it shows the pages of the blog;
- **single.php**: this is the file that handles the display of a single page ("page" is intended as specific feature of WordPress);
- **comments.php**: it performs the function of displaying the comments for a blog post, along with the form to send new comments. This file is called from the file single.php;
- **header.php**: this file handles the display of the blog's header;
- **footer.php**: it manages the contents located into blog's Footer;
- **sidebar.php**: it manages content in the blog's sidebar (or sidebars, if more than one);
- **search.php**: this is the page opened when users make a search among the contents of the blog;
- **functions.php**: this is the file that contains functions of the theme, written by those who have developed it;
- **style.css**: this is one of the most important files of theme. The stylesheet is used to determine how different elements of the web pages should be shown (color, dimensions, alignment, etc.).

Obviously, there can be other files, in addition to those listed here. For example, in some themes, where there is the possibility to manage multiple sidebars to obtain a 3-column layout, there can be two distinct files, one for the left sidebar and the other for the right one.

To edit these files, you must have appropriate knowledge of PHP, HTML, as well as management style sheets (cascade stylesheets, or CSS).

Since there are topic that transcend the scope of this book, we not go into detail of aspects concerning the WordPress editor.

However, if you have this type of knowledge, it is clear that it will be possible to use this tool for you, however paying much attention, because when you modify these files, also an apparently banal error can cause dramatic problems, on the blog.

Chapter 9 - Other elements of WordPress

WordPress: not only posts and pages

The most important part of a blog is certainly represented by the posts, by the pages and by the comments left by our users. That is, all those elements concerning, in practice, contents of the blog itself.

In addition to these elements, a blog has other auxiliary functions that, if fully exploited, can provide a huge added value for blog, allowing it to grow and differentiate itself from many other blogs available on the Internet.

Therefore, in this chapter we will see some of the most important features, considering that their use is not mandatory, although strongly recommended because of the benefits that it can bring to our blog.

The useful features that we examine in the next few pages are mainly the following: the media library, the blogroll and, the last but not the least, the feed and syndication system.

Media Library

In Chapter 5 we saw how it is possible to insert an image into a post, simply by using the "Add Media" button.

However, we can need, once image is uploaded, to replace it with another or to delete it, perhaps to preserve the space included in the web hosting plan that we paid.

In these cases, the section for managing the media may be useful, because it allows us to manage all our multimedia files embedded in posts and pages with several features, like the ability to change title, alternate text (used to get a blog with a good accessibility level, for users with vision problem, who open HTML pages with text only browsers), caption and description.

The Media Library is accessible via the menu "Media". In particular, WordPress currently provides two submenus:
- **Add New**: to upload a new multimedia file;
- **Library**: to manage already uploaded multimedia files.

Since in Chapter 5 we inserted an image into a post (in our blog), we can see this image in the media library, by clicking on the second menu item.

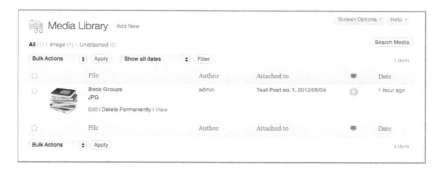

We can note that, as usual, placing the mouse pointer on the title of one of the images (in our case, the only image we uploaded), some links appear. They are useful to change image properties, or for removal and display of itself.

Furthermore, on the same screen we can see what's the post at which the image is connected. This is very useful to know if the image is actually utilized on the blog or not. In the latter case, we can decide to remove it, and increase the total amount of available web space for our blog.

Links and blogroll

One of the most favorite elements of a WordPress blog is, from the point of view of bloggers (especially when starting it), the blogroll, also known as "friend list".

The blogroll is an element that may exist or not within a blog.

It is simply a list of links to websites.

Usually, it is located within a sidebar and is easily activated and configured via a specific widget, following procedure explained in Chapter 8, concerning management of the look and feel of the blog.

In practice, if we want to insert, in our blog, a section such as "useful links", we can use this tool.

The criteria for deciding what links have to be entered in the blogroll can be extremely varied.

On some blogs, blogroll is used to contain the list of all the websites that treat the same topics and / or other reference websites.

In other cases, especially for personal blog, blogroll is used just like a list of friend sites and / or other websites followed closely by its bloggers.

In short, there is no clear rule, it all depends on personal taste and motivations of the owner of the blog.

In many circumstances, the blogroll is also used as a tool to establish relationships with other bloggers.

For example, just to report a personal experience, when SPACE 4 TUTORIAL blog was born, back in (but not too much) 2007, I sent an email to some other bloggers (computer enthusiasts, as me). On that occasion, through agreements with each of them, I made a mutual exchange of links in the blogroll.

So, in the blogroll of SPACE 4 TUTORIAL were inserted links to their blogs and, vice versa, in the blogrolls on these other bloggers, was added a link to the home page of SPACE 4 TUTORIAL.

This use of blogroll has a huge advantage from the point of view of inclusion in search engines, that is often unknown to most new bloggers and also some expert webmasters.

In fact, by using the blogroll as a tool to create relationships with other bloggers and to receive inbound links from other websites, a blogger allows its own blog to appear on major search engines since the early days of online presence of it.

This is due to the inner workings of search engines, which, during the analysis of a single web page, will scan all the links contained within it, looking for new pages linked, in cascade.

This means that if the link to our blog is already on an indexed website, when search engine's crawlers analyze links within a page of the website (for example, just those in the blogroll), they will also find the link to our blog and they will begin to index our pages.

So, with a correct use of blogroll, we can appear on search engines very quickly and, at the same time, we can immediately obtain back-links, which offer advantages in terms of positioning and PageRank (although the importance of the latter, recently, has been reduced a bit, compared to the past).

Given the advantages offered by the presence of a blogroll, we will see in practice how to handle it in our blog and how to add some links.

Within the WordPress administration panel, let's select the menu "Links" → "All Links". In this way, we can see a list of all the links that are already in our blogroll:

Links	Add New				Screen Options ▾	Help ▾
						Search Links
Bulk Actions ⬍ Apply	View all categories ⬍ Filter					
☐ Name	URL	Categories	Relationship	Visible	Rating	
☐ Documentation Edit I Delete Edit "Documentation"	codex.wordpress.org	Blogroll		Yes	0	
☐ Feedback	wordpress.org/support/forum/requ...	Blogroll		Yes	0	
☐ Plugins	wordpress.org/extend/plugins	Blogroll		Yes	0	
☐ Support Forums	wordpress.org/support	Blogroll		Yes	0	
☐ Themes	wordpress.org/extend/themes	Blogroll		Yes	0	
☐ WordPress Blog	wordpress.org/news	Blogroll		Yes	0	
☐ WordPress Planet	planet.wordpress.org	Blogroll		Yes	0	
☐ Name	URL	Categories	Relationship	Visible	Rating	
Bulk Actions ⬍ Apply						

As we can see, during the installation process, some default links, relative to some reference sites for WordPress, were automatically inserted. However, we can modify and/or delete them, at any time, using the special links "Edit" and "Delete" available in correspondence with each link.

To add a new link, however, let's use the "Add New", located on the top of the page, or alternatively the menu "Links" → "Add New".

Let's suppose, for example, we want to add a link to the main blog of SPACE 4 TUTORIAL (a random blog! Obviously, if you decide to add a link to this blog, please let me know, so I will do the same and you will be on search engines within a very short time).

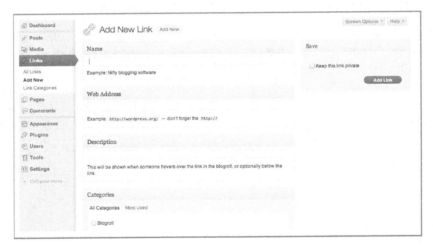

Options on this page are very intuitive.

In the "**Name**" field, let's enter a name that we want to appear with the link on the blogroll. In our case, we are inserting the text "Space 4 Tutorial".

In the "**Web Address**" field let's insert URL, that is the link to website: http://www.space4tutorial.com.

In the "**Description**" field, let's insert some text to describe website. This description, according to the theme used and the settings of the widget "Links" (when used to reveal the blogroll in the sidebar of the blog), can be shown under the name of link, in the blogroll.

Regarding the panel dedicated to "**Category**", we must first point out that the links loaded through the "Links" menu of administrative panel may eventually be grouped, as needed.

Personally, I rarely use this kind of grouping, because I don't often have to distinguish the links by category. However, if you need to manage more than one category of links (because they might use more than one widget to contain links to different kind of websites), then you can select, within this field, the categories of membership for links that you are entering and / or add new ones, using the "Add New Category", or via the menu item "Links" → "Link Categories".

Otherwise, we can select the default category "Blogroll".

Instead, the field "**Destination**" allows us to determine the window where contents of the link have to be displayed when a user clicks on it. Options are "_blank - new window or tab", "_top - current window or tab, with no frames", and "_none - same window or tab".

The next panel is titled "**Link Relationship (XFN)**". It comes from the idea of representing, through hyperlinks, human relations that exist between two websites.

In fact, XFN stands for XHTML Friends Network and, in practice, this option allows us to indicate, within the XHTML code, the kind of relationship between the persons who own two blogs linked together by links contained in this blogroll.

For those who know HTML, this relationship is represented by the attribute rel = "", located inside the tag of the various links <a href>.

In our example, if we select the relationship of friendship "friend", among several options provided by WordPress, then within the html code concerning the blogroll we will find a tag as <a href = "http://www.space4tutorial.com/" rel="friend">.

Instead, in the "**Advanced**" box, we can find more options, like the ability to associate an image with each link, as well as an URL concerning the RSS feed (in the next section we go into detail of feeds and syndication), annotations and a score.

Once we enter these options (not all of them are required, but usually at least the first three should be used), we can click on the "Add Link", found on the top-right corner of screen.

In the same pane, there is the option "Keep this link private".

This option, when selected, allows us to save the link without showing it to users of the blog.

After adding the link, we can view the blog.

But we need to add the "Links" widget to the sidebar as shown in the paragraph "The Widgets" in Chapter 8, concerning the look and feel of the blog.

Among the options, if we need it, we can also select the one concerning the description of the links, as you can see in the screenshot below:

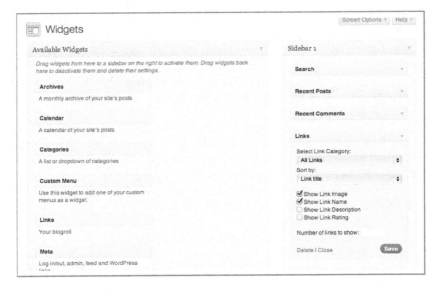

After adding the widget, we can see the blogroll, with the new link, that we just added.

Placing the mouse pointer over the link, we will also see a description of the link, shown to us through an easy tooltip (contextual hint):

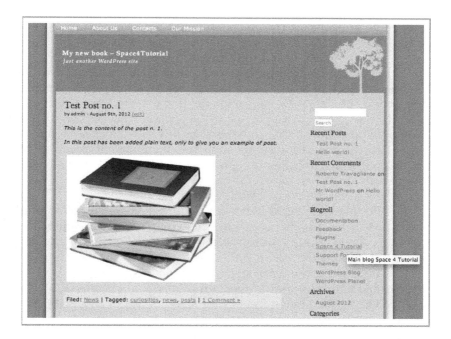

The RSS and ATOM feeds

Another element of particular importance in maintaining a blog, is formed by Feed.

How many times have you ever run into strange messages like: "Subscribe to feed", "Subscribe", or "Subscribe to RSS" and similar?

How many times have you wondered what those entries meant?

If you do not have the pleasure to know them, the feeds are, from the perspective of end users, a useful and convenient way to retrieve Internet contents (web contents) from multiple websites (sources), without being forced to view all of them, one by one.

In practice, feeds are a simple but very powerful system to get all the updates that affect your favorite websites.

With traditional web navigation, if you read the contents from multiple websites (for example news, reviews, etc.), then you must have access, by using your browser (Internet Explorer, Firefox, Safari, etc ...), to every interesting websites, one by one.

For example, if we want to know if there are new posts on "Space 4 Tutorial" or "Il Bloggatore", we must first enter the link http://www.space4tutorial.com and see if there are news, then re-enter the link http://www.ilbloggatore.com and do the same thing. All these activities waste time, from the point of view of the end users.

If we are visiting two websites, these activities are very simple, but if the websites become 10, or 20, or 50, then we could spend many hours just to see if there are new posts.

So, what can we do? Well, we can use to feed!

For more technical users, feeds are web contents enclosed in small XML files. In practice, with feed system and feed readers, we can subscribe to multiple websites and we can get, at any time and in a moment, all updates from them.

With feeds, users can stay tuned about updates from 10, 100 or 1000 and more websites, without effort.

The most common formats for feeds are RSS and ATOM. We will not dwell on the technical differences, as they are not relevant for the purposes of this book. But you must know that the majority of feed readers is able to read both formats, in their different versions.

Generally, on a website or blog where feeds are enabled there is a link to them, usually accompanied by an image like this:

Other times, you can find expressions such as "Subscribe to our feeds", "Atom feeds", "RSS", "Subscribe", and so on.

Moreover, if we use one of the latest versions of Internet Explorer, Mozilla Firefox, or Safari, we can see this orange icon, or others with similar meaning, located into the address bar or toolbar and, by clicking on it, we can access the feed of the current website.

The easiest way to read feeds (both RSS and ATOM) is by using a feed reader. Some feed readers allows you also to group multiple feeds by categories, according to the different websites that you wish to follow.

The most common browsers, like Internet Explorer, Mozilla Firefox, or Safari, include feed reader functionalities, so you can store several RSS/ATOM links, in a manner similar to Bookmarks or Favorites. For example, Mozilla Firefox calls them "Live Bookmarks", just to indicate that these contents are updated dynamically.

Alternatively, you can use a specific feed reader, also running as an online application. For example, you can use Google Reader.

In any case, a feed reader allows you to store multiple RSS/Atom links and shows updates related to different websites and blogs on a regular basis, in a manner similar to management of e-mail with Outlook Express, Mozilla Thunderbird, or Evolution.

Thunderbird, for example, in addition to its normal features as mail client software, also provides a RSS reader.

In practice, a feed is made up of a XML stream containing the posts of the blog, that are organized according to a well defined structure. This structure allows easy reading from a multitude of devices, with very different hardware.

In fact, as feed is composed by standard XML, it can be fed with feed reader designed for mobile devices without too many problems, or it can be used as a means to get updates from a blog or, again, to make web contents very interoperable between different platforms.

For example, here is the feed for SPACE 4 TUTORIAL as seen by Mozilla Firefox:

again, here is the same content, processed through a feed reader installed on a mobile device:

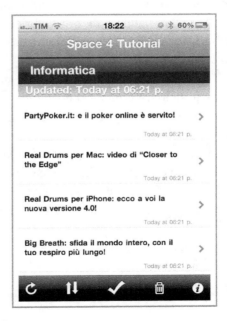

With regard to WordPress, inside the administration panel we can find several options about feed management.

In fact, by using the menu "Settings" → "Reading", we can reach a page where we can define the number of posts displayed into the feed and the type of encoding (UTF-8 is generally recommended).

We can also decide if the contents of each post must be reported in complete or preview format.

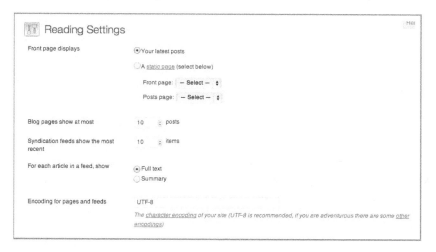

It's important to note that WordPress supports several types of standard formats for feeds and, in particular, the most common: RSS 2.0, Atom 1.0 and RSS 0.92.

These feeds are reachable, usually, by using URL like the following:

- http://www.blogname.com/?feed=rss2
- http://www.blogname.com/?feed=atom
- http://www.blogname.com/?feed=rss

Or, if we use a structure other than the default permalinks (see Chapter 12):

- http://www.blogname.com/feed/

- http://www.blogname.com/feed/atom/
- http://www.blogname.com/feed/rss/

Beyond the specific differences, in technical terms, about these different types of standards, the fact of supporting multiple formats allows a WordPress blog to be browsed using practically any type of feed reader.

Feeds and Aggregators

Feeds are a very important feature of a WordPress blog also because they give the blogger an opportunity to get the better propagation for its contents.

More precisely, they are a powerful promotional tool when put in relation to the presence of a particular kind of websites, available on the Internet: web content aggregators.

Web aggregators are portals that constantly fetch feed from several blogs in order to and make their content available to the widest range of people. In practice, the feeds from these blogs (usually referred as SOURCE) are imported and analyzed by a software ("syndication engine") that parses and extracts their content, and incorporate it within the pages of the aggregator.

A web content aggregator, usually, has a role of "collector", relatively to a particular type of content.

The main purpose is to provide a unique channel that allows readers to get news from different sources in a very short time.

There are many web aggregators on the Internet, but the example that I can report to you with the greatest enthusiasm is certainly the one that I founded some years ago (January 1, 2008): "Il Bloggatore" (http://www.ilbloggatore.com). It was born as online aggregator related to computer science, but today it is oriented also towards the development of other new channels (kitchen, television, sports, marketing, and more).

Not all web aggregators bring real benefits to your own blog, so when you register your blog, you need to evaluate all the different features they offer to registered blogs.

In particular, to distinguish the best web aggregators from others, I suggest to consider only those that:

- show only preview of posts (so, users are encouraged to read the full article on the original blog, that is ours, referred as SOURCE);
- show, for each syndicated and analyzed post, at least a link to the blog source (not "nofollow", as this type of link offers no benefits from the point of view of the presence on the search engines);
- doesn't include costs for aggregation (or provides limited cost, in relation to any additional services offered to blog's members).

Personally, I consider very important the inclusion of a blog to one or more online aggregators. Although the opinion about this kind of portals is not unanimous, I believe that if you create a blog today, web content aggregators can be a great way to promote it, in a generally free manner. Moreover, they can be a good way to immediately see your blog in the major search engines.

Chapter 10 - Plugins

WordPress' flexibility

As we saw in the previous chapters, WordPress has, in addition to typical features of a platform for the creation of blogs, other accessory modules that allow us to realize not only blogs, but also high quality business websites.

Everything without any effort from the webmaster!

Furthermore, WordPress has a great capacity for expansion and flexibility, by the support of additional specially designed components, called plugins.

What's a plugin?

Basically, a plugin is an add-on that allows us to add features to WordPress and perform many different tasks. It is composed of one or more .PHP files, containing the code of the plugin itself, and possibly, other useful files.

There is no limit to the possibilities offered by plugins. And it's no coincidence that there are many plugins already developed for the different versions of WordPress, allowing us to do everything.

During the implementation phase of our blog, we can use one or more plugins for some of the features we need. Also, anytime we can add and remove plugins, with a few clicks, without change our blog radically.

This is a very important aspect concerning management of a WordPress blog, since the life of blogger is extremely simplified and allows the latter to focus more time on writing contents, rather than on the purely technical elements that website creation usually involves.

Since there are many plugins available online, we could never analyze in detail all of them. Therefore, for instructions about use of each of them, please, refer to the documentation prepared by the respective developers.

In these pages, however, we will see mainly how to install plugins and their removal (if you need).

Furthermore, we will report a list of top common plugins, along with a brief description of the respective features provided.

Installing e configuring plugins

As we will see in this section, the installation of a plugin is not very different from installation of a theme for WordPress.

Also in this case we can proceed in two ways:

*   by using exclusively the WordPress administration panel;
*   by using a software for file transfer via FTP, within our web space as we have already seen for themes, with the only difference that the destination directory for plugins is *"wp-content/plugins/"* and not *"wp-content/themes/"*.

However, unlike themes, many of the plugins available on the Internet are also in the repository managed by the official website of WordPress (http://wordpress.org/extend/plugins/).

Therefore, at least for the most common features, it is almost always possible to use the installation procedure reachable from the administrative panel of WordPress, without consider all the other technical aspects.

The section dedicated to the plugins can be reached, as usual, from the administrative panel, via the menu item "Plugins".

From here, we can view a list concerning all plugins that are currently installed on our blog. In a similar manner to the themes, even the plugin must be activated and for this reason, in this page, we can also display only inactive plugins.

Clicking on the menu item "Installed Plugins", within the sample blog that we are creating, there are two plugins: Akismet and Hello Dolly:

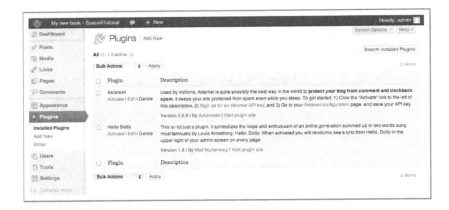

These are two plugins included in the default installation of WordPress. The first, Akismet, is responsible for the management of SPAM comments and can be used to delete all comments containing unsolicited advertising, very similar to what happens for the most popular systems for email management.

The second one, Hello Dolly, as stated in the description that accompanies it, is not exactly a plugin but a symbol of hope and enthusiasm of an entire generation, that is summed up in a song by Louis Armstrong. This song is titled with just two words: Hello Dolly, precisely. This is a plugin that randomly shows the phrases of this song in the top right corner of the blog and we usually don't need to activate it, because this plugin does not add other features.

Both plugins are disabled and can be activated at any time by clicking on the link "Activate". Moreover, both these and other plugins that we will install, may be removed by simply using the "Delete" link.

Moreover, again from this screen or, alternatively, by using the sub-menu "Add new", we can install new plugins, in relation to the features that we wish to add to our blog.

In this section, we will see how to install one of the many plugins that are available online. Among them, we will chose the one that implements mobile viewing within our blog, to allow users to easily see our blog even if they are using a smartphone or an other mobile device.

To do this, let's click on "Add new", cited above. It's important to note that WordPress, without a plugin specifically activated in it (unless the theme does also support the "mobile viewing" as option), does not care whether the type of device used by the visitor of the blog is a PC or a mobile phone or a tablet.

So whether we are accessing the blog via a PC, or we are doing the same thing by using a mobile device, we will see a page with the same appearance.

For example, here's what we'll see with a mobile device like the Apple iPhone:

Even with a smartphone equipped with the Android operating system (for "par condicio") the blog is not very different:

Let's keep in mind these two screens, because the plugins that we are going to install will change the normal behavior of WordPress, allowing us to view the posts of the blog with a different layout, more appropriate to the tiny screen of a smartphone.

By clicking on the menu "Plugins" → "Add New", we get the following screen, where we can search and install a new plugin:

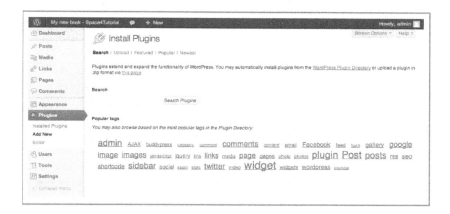

Since the WordPress plugins that add support for mobile viewing are so many, we will use the search text box available in this page, and we will choose one of them.

As, at present, the most popular smartphones are devices which run the IOS operating system of Apple (we are referring to the iPhone, iPod Touch and iPad) and those equipped with the Google Android OS, we'll conduct a targeted search, by inserting the words "iPhone" and "Android" in this text box.

By clicking the "Search Plugins" button, we get a list consisting of all the plugins, in the repository of WordPress.org , meeting our search criteria.

Of course, not all of these plugins perform the function that we want to implement in our blog. Some of them, in fact, appear within the search results only because they have, in the title or description, at least one the keywords used for search. For example, the plugin called "Piggy" appears in the list, but performs a totally different task, concerning the ability to view blog's statistics by using an iPhone or an Android device.

Next to each plugin, there are two links: "Details" and "Install Now". The first one shows us some information about the plugin, as the screenshots, the level of compatibility with different versions of WordPress, the link to developer's website, etc..

Moreover, in the same screen, we can find the current version of the plugin, along with a score based on the evaluations left by users who have already used the plugin, as well as a brief description.

Instead, the link "Install Now" allows us to begin installing the plugin.

As far as our practical example, we will install a plugin called "WordPress PDA & iPhone." There are many other plugins that perform the same tasks, so it should be noted that we choose this rather than other similar only because it appears, at the time of this writing, on the first page of results and it has a good rating (4 out of 5 stars).

Therefore, let's click on "Install Now", at the plugin "WordPress PDA & iPhone". There will appear a confirmation request and we must respond "OK".

At this point, the installation of the plugin starts. When finished, the plugin will be activated and we will get a confirmation page.

To make sure that everything is ok, we can return on the page of installed plugins (menu "Plugins" → "Installed Plugins"). Here's our screen:

As we can see, the plugin has been installed and it is enabled.

In addition, within the "Plugins" menu appeared another menu item, "PDA", introduced by the newly installed plugin.

This is a very important aspect of WordPress plugins, namely the ability to create new menu items and / or other features within the administrative panel.

The addition of a new menu item by plugins, generally gives the possibility to blogger to configure the plugin itself, according to its functions.

In this case, if we click on the new submenu "PDA", we get a screen that does not correspond to a native page of WordPress. In fact, this page has just added by the installed plugin to allow the latter to set the types of browsers for which the "mobile" display must be activated:

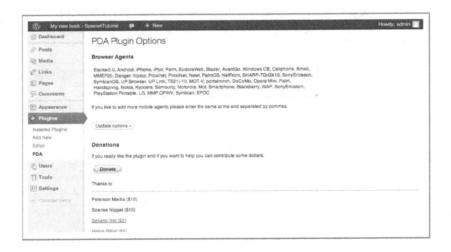

By activating this plugin, we have just added support for mobile viewing to our blog. Therefore, from this moment, if we browse the blog by using a mobile phone, we can view its contents with the typical layout of a mobile site.

Here's the appearance of our blog, if we connect to it via a smartphone like the iPhone:

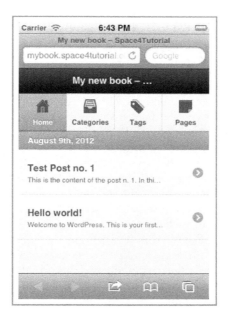

Essential Plugins

An infinity of other plugins (performing many different tasks) is available on the Internet and, in particular, by the repository where we found the WordPress plugin to support mobile devices.

Among the over 18.000 plugins currently available only in the official repository, there are some that, usually, I recommend for a blog, because of features that provide.

Therefore, below is a short list (with brief description) of some plugins that can help us for some of the most common needs that may arise during design and implementation of a blog.

- **Akismet**: As already mentioned in the previous paragraph, this is a default plugin installed with WordPress. It covers the management of SPAM comments received from our blog users and, in particular, to eliminate them, automatically. To activate this plugin you need an API Key, that we can get by registering quickly to this website: http://akismet.com.

- **All in One SEO Pack**: a plugin that takes care of optimizing the blog in relation to major search engines. This plugin offers a range of options that allow a very direct management of HTML meta tags. It is constantly updated by developer, according to changes concerning the several supported search engines.
- **Google XML Sitemap**: it is responsible for the generation of a XML sitemap concerning our blog. This sitemap contains a list of all the links of the blogs that we want to index for search engines and it can be automatically generated and fed to the search engines to speed up the indexing of web contents.
- **Contact Form**: this is a plugin that allows us to insert a form within a post or page, so users can interact with us. User's messages received via this plugin are forwarded to bloggers via email.
- **WP-Polls**: plugin which enables the implementation of surveys on the blog.
- **Add to Any: Share / Bookmark / Email Buttons**: Plugin for adding, at each blog post, some buttons useful for social bookmarking, or for sharing via several "social" channels as facebook, twitter, and so on...
- **FeedStats**: useful plugin that provides useful statistics on feed users.
- **Mingle - Users - Online**: plugin that provides statistics concerning the number of users who visit our blog.

It's important to repeat that online there are other plugins that perform the same tasks of those listed above, so just search a little to display all the alternatives, directly from the WordPress administration panel.

Editor

In a similar way to management of themes, WordPress makes available to the bloggers an appropriate editor for management of plugins.

This means that we can act on individual files that make up each plugin directly via the administration panel (of course, only if we know the PHP language).

To access the editor, we can use the menu *"Plugins"* → *"Editor"*.

However, in general, the use of this editor to modify the code of installed plugins should not be necessary and, in any case, to modify files that compose them it is important to have good knowledge of PHP and HTML, as well as CSS (cascade stylesheets).

Since PHP, HTML and CSS are topics that transcend the scope of this book, we will not expand on aspects of using the WordPress editor. However, if you have this kind of knowledge, you can use this tool paying much attention, because when you work directly on these files, also a trivial error can cause very serious problems about the normal running of the blog.

Chapter 11 - Users and Security

Blog and Users

One of the aspects which need careful consideration, especially when designing our blog, concerns the handling of users who will have access to it.

In particular, we refer not only visitors to the blog (loyal or occasional), but also those who will play an active part of our project.

For example, if we are going to create a business blog, we must consider whether it should be updated only by a person or more users and in the latter case, we must ask ourselves "who does what?", that is to establish the different roles that we want to assign to each person who accesses the administrative panel of the blog.

Of course, for most of personal blogs there is not this kind of problem, since each operation is usually performed by the owner, with the default user profile.

In fact, during the first installation, WordPress automatically creates an administrative user, called "admin". This user can be considered the super-user of WordPress, since it can perform any type of operation within the blog.

User management becomes essential for blogs that are characterized by a collective management and an "editorial" organization, where some persons write posts, while others deal of their revision and approval, to publish them on the blog.

Regarding external visitors, in addition, user management can allow to make certain content available only to persons who are registered on the blog.

For example, WordPress allows you to limit the display of pages and / or posts to registered users only. In fact, among the options available within the section for creating a post or a WordPress page, we can find the specific option concerning the visibility to be given to related web content:

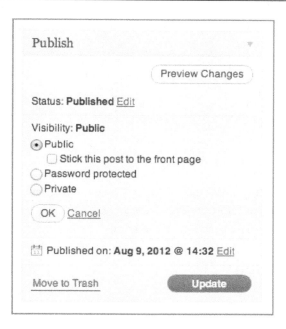

There are three options:

- **Public**: the post (or page) can be accessed by everyone;
- **Password protected**: the post (or page) can be viewed only by those who enter a password. Clicking on this option, a text box appears where to enter the password;
- **Private**: the post (or page) is accessible only by registered users.

Furthermore, within the configuration page related to comments that we saw in Chapter 7 ("Settings" → "Discussion"), there are several options concerning user management. For example, there is an option which limits the ability to write comments only to registered users of the blog. Moreover, we can find option to bind comments to approval by users with an administrative profile.

Other comment settings	☑ Comment author must fill out name and e-mail
	☐ Users must be registered and logged in to comment
	☐ Automatically close comments on articles older than 14 ⟐ days
	☑ Enable threaded (nested) comments 5 ⟐ levels deep
	☐ Break comments into pages with 50 ⟐ top level comments per page and the last ⟐ page displayed by default
	Comments should be displayed with the older ⟐ comments at the top of each page
E-mail me whenever	☑ Anyone posts a comment
	☑ A comment is held for moderation
Before a comment appears	☐ An administrator must always approve the comment
	☑ Comment author must have a previously approved comment

Given the potential value of user management in certain situations, in this short chapter we will see how to add and configure new users and the various profiles that can be assigned to each one.

User creation

To create a user in WordPress, we use the administration panel, and, more precisely, we access the "Users" menu item.

In particular, we can use the menu "Users" → "All Users" to access the list of users currently registered on our blog and then, we can click on "Add New", or directly choose the submenu "Add New", on the left side of administrative panel.

The form that appears allows us to create a new user, entering various information, such as username, email address, first and last name, any web site url and a password. There is also a password strength indicator.

Moreover, in this page there is the option to send password for a user via email, and the role to assign to the latter.

In fact, in a blog with multiple users often we need to establish relationships on what each can do, namely its permissions.

Permissions and Roles

When a blog is handled by several persons, inevitably, there is the need to establish an organization that allows the best possible management of information.

In this perspective, the blog takes an "editorial" structure similar to that concerning a newspaper organization, where a distinction is made between those who produce posts, those who moderates them, who manages the look and feel, and so on.

To allow this, WordPress provides a user management articulated on multiple profiles, known as "roles", which identify the function of each person who works at the blogs and, consequently, permissions.

The roles provided natively in WordPress are five and their management is quite simple, because it's designed to use WordPress as a blogging platform by any type of blogger, by the newbie to more experienced.

However, on the Internet there are several plugins that extend the standard management of permissions and roles, and add various security features, so it is possible, at any time, installing one of them according to specific requirements.

The roles provided by the WordPress team are the following:

- **Administrator**: the administrative user of the blog, it can do almost everything on the blog, such as writing new posts, installing themes and plugins, moderating comments, managing users and profiles, and so on. In short, it can access all the features available in the WordPress administrative panel.
- **Editor**: it can create new posts (and pages) and modify the posts created by other users. It can also moderate comments left by blog's readers, and modify categories. Unlike the administrator user that can change profile of all other users, the editor can edit only its own profile.
- **Author**: the author can only edit its own profile. Moreover, it can create and publish only posts. It can't act on posts created by other users, but it can change or remove its own posts.
- **Contributor**: it can act on its own profile and write only posts. However, it can't publish them. Publishing must be made by an editor or an administrator.
- **Subscriber**: the subscriber can edit its own profile and access the dashboard only to consultation purposes.

The role of a user is typically established during the its creation, but it is not excluded that it may subsequently change. For example, it may happen that, in a blog run by an organizational structure similar to that of a real newspaper, we want to change a user's role from "author" to "editor".

In this case, in the page concerning user management (menu "Users" → "All users"), we can just click on the link "Edit" where we want to change the user's role and, finally, we can select the role we want to give the user.

To demonstrate all this with a practical example, let's create a user "userbook" using the menu item "Add New":

Next, let's try and change this newly created user, by changing its role from "Author" to "Editor". Let's click on the link "Edit" related to the newly created user and let's use the handy combo box concerning the role:

After creating the user "userbook", we can access to WordPress with the new account information. To do this, let's logout from the WordPress administrative panel, because we are currently logged as "admin".

Let's click on the greeting at the top right corner ("Hello admin") and we will see a drop down menu, where there is an entry "Logout".

By selecting this entry, we can disconnect from the WordPress admin panel:

Next, let's access by using the newly created username and password:

At this point, once again access to WordPress, we can notice that some menu items are no longer available. For example, we will not find the menus about management of plugins or themes. This is because we are not logged as administrator, but as normal users in the role of editor and the ability to install and / or remove plugins and themes is allowed only to the administrator of the blog.

In particular, having the role of Editor, we will find only the enabled menu items "Posts", "Media", "Comments", "Profile" and "Tools".

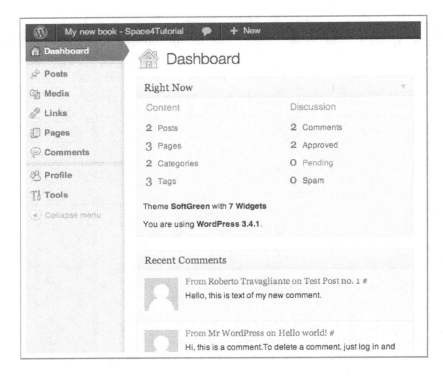

Security and the importance of updating

The security of a WordPress blog is not limited to a more or less effective management of users, but it must be realized through a series of stratagems designed to remove those factors that may allow unauthorized access by third parties and, therefore, that can undermine the correct functionality of the blog.

In this perspective, it is important to keep your installation up to date with the latest versions of WordPress.

After all, WordPress is nothing but a web application that makes some contents accessible to users through a web server and, as such, has all the security issues that normally plague web software.

This means that WordPress is not immune to all these types of attacks that point to web sites like, just to name a few, SQL injection, attacks related to the HTTP protocol, buffer overflow attacks concerning specific parts of WordPress code, attacks to web server that runs the blog, and so on.

It is not uncommon, from companies specialized in computer security, finding new vulnerabilities that an attacker can use to compromise the system where it is running our blog.

To confirm this, just type in any search engine the phrase "wordpress vulnerabilities".

You will see several websites that treat vulnerabilities about WordPress and some of its most popular plugins. These bugs can be exploited for different purposes (for example, to attack the server that runs our blog, to use the system that hosts our blog as a beachhead for further attacks directed to other computer systems, for "deface" of our website, etc.).

Generally, as it is for other software products, if it's discovered that a version of WordPress has some security vulnerabilities, the development team tries to correct parts of the PHP code that cause problems and, when the necessary corrections are available, it prepares a new version of CMS, downloadable by users.

Hence the need to keep updated our installation of WordPress.

If we installed, for example, version 3.0 of WordPress, which has one or more vulnerabilities and we don't update to later versions (where these vulnerabilities are removed), we risk leaving our blog unprotected from attacks by any cracker who can successfully exploit these vulnerabilities. And, regardless of whether the attacker does so to take possession of our server and/or simply to "deface" our website, we allow anyone to disturb the normal operation of our blog.

It must be emphasized that the need to constantly update the software is not just about WordPress, but also concerns the various plugins and the rest of the software installed on the server.

Obviously, unless we bought a completely self-managed dedicated server, we can only act on WordPress and plugins, while the rest of the software on the server must be constantly updated by the service provider.

Updating WordPress

To help keeping our blogging platform up to date, WordPress provides a semi-automatic update system that alerts us when a new update is available. It allows us to update both WordPress and installed themes and plugins.

This system was introduced in version 2.7 and has greatly simplified updates, compared to the past.

In fact, for version prior to 2.7, a more complex procedure was necessary. This procedure can be summed, substantially, in the following steps:

- replacement of all of WordPress php files, except that relating to the configuration ("wp-config.php") and those contained in the folder "wp-content", regarding the themes, plugins and media inserted in posts and pages;
- execution of a script set up by the WordPress team, to update the database structure in relation to the new version to install.

Due to the greater complexity of this method of updating WordPress, for which it is necessary an FTP client to copy the files on our web space and, however, a better technical knowledge, starting from version 2.7, the WordPress development team has introduced a new upgrade system, which automatically handles all of these steps.

Furthermore, this system also handles updates of plugins and it is accessible directly from the WordPress administrative panel, via a few clicks.

For example, while writing this book, I realized that the blog SPACE 4 TUTORIAL (http://www.space4tutorial.com) need to be updated to the latest release, yet.

That's the way WordPress warns me about the need to update, directly from the dashboard:

Please, note that my blog SPACE 4 TUTORIAL is localized in Italian. So, the following screenshots will show a WordPress configured for Italian language.

However, In the following pages, I'll indicate buttons, links and other elements of WordPress, by using the equivalent English words.

Well, after this clarification, let's go on!

I must just click on the "Update Now" link to launch the update process, which will guide me in all of next steps.

In addition, on the menu on the left, there is an entry "Updates", which tells me that there are 6 updates to be made on the blog. What are they? To find out, I click on this menu item, right now.

As we have said, WordPress not only deals updates to the "core", but also updates concerning plugins.

The following screenshot confirms it.

Indeed, it is showing first that the WordPress "core" can be updated to a recent version:

In addition, within the same screen, the plugins that require an update are listed. In particular, right now, on my blog there are the Akismet plugin (for the management of spam comments) and All in One SEO Pack (for SEO):

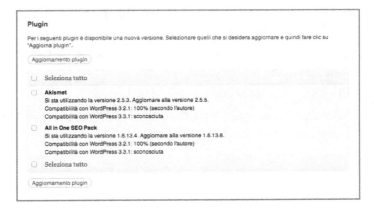

Finally, in the same screen, deeper, we can see the themes for which there is an updated version:

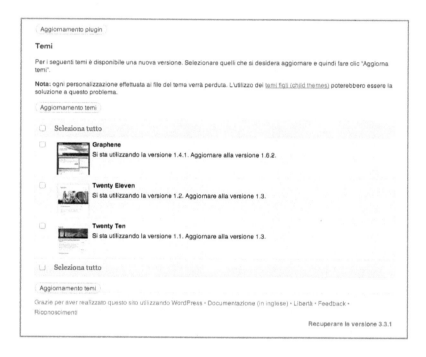

To update each of these items, we can just select the appropriate box (checkbox) and click on the update button.

For example, we decide to update Akismet. Let's check at the Akismet plugin and let's click on the button "Update Plugin". Here is what appears:

As you can see, the only update for the Akismet plugin has been completed. We can do the same for all other plugins, themes and the "core" of WordPress.

Of course, the fact that WordPress provides a very simple procedure for the update, does not exempt us from performing a backup of database and files every time we make updates (at least for the most important ones, affecting rather than individual WordPress plugins and themes).

In fact, when performing this kind of operations, it can always happen the unpredictable and, in this case, it is better to be prepared, with a backup that can allow us to recover our posts, pages and other elements of our blog.

Chapter 12 - The Settings

A comfortable menu to manage the blog

Within a few years, WordPress has conquered thousands and thousands of bloggers, thanks to its flexibility and its enormous potential. Today, it can be considered one of the best platform, not only for blogging, but also for creating business and company websites.

However, what makes WordPress a great platform, is certainly its immense simplicity. In fact, with WordPress, you can set various options about the configuration of the blog.

In particular, to edit all main settings of our blog, WordPress provides a handy menu "Settings". We already mentioned it in previous chapters and, in these pages, we will see it in more detail, exploring its submenus.

More precisely, the entries in the settings, where we can intervene to change the behavior and the various aspects of our blog, are:

- General
- Writing
- Reading
- Discussion
- Media
- Privacy
- Permalinks

Below there is description about the features performed by each of these items.

Generally, a blogger configures it after the installation of the blog and usually do not change then.

General

This page covers all the general settings regarding the blog.
In particular, it leads to a page where we can define:
- **blog title**, defined during the first installation;
- **the tagline**, consisting of a slogan for the blog;
- **URLs** concerning WordPress and site addresses;
- **Email address** to send notifications related to the blog. This email address usually coincides with the administrator's email;
- the possibility or not, for users, to register themselves to the blog;
- the default role for users who register on the blog themselves;
- time zone and format of date and time, to be used to show dates and hours at the posts.

Writing

This section covers some settings especially useful when entering web content to our blog, such as posts and pages.

Among the options available in this section, we can find:
- the number of lines displayed in the box used for writing posts;
- a checkbox for the conversion of characters sequences such as :-) and ;-D into graphical emoticons;
- a checkbox to automatically correct the XHTML incorrectly nested;
- the indication of the default category for posts ("Uncategorized");
- the indication of the default category for links ("Blogroll");
- the ability to configure the bookmarklet "Press This". This is a small application that allows us to easily create, through our browser, the posts from scraps of web pages;

- the ability to configure sending posts via email. This feature allows to publish posts directly by sending an email to a secret mailbox. Each received email is automatically published on the blog;
- the ability to enable Atom Publishing Protocol and XML-RPC.

Reading

This section contains options concerning consultation of the blog by users:

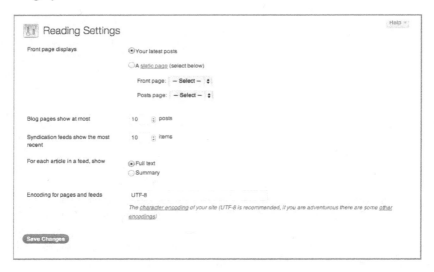

The options on this page allow us to determine:
- what must be the first page to display, in particular whether it should be a static page, or the list of recent posts;
- the number of posts to display, for each page;
- the number of posts to display in the blog feed;
- if posts must be displayed in preview or full mode, when user reads the feed;
- the type of encoding to use for the pages of the blog.

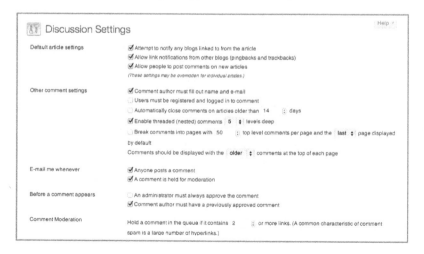

Discussion

We already saw this page in Chapter 7, dedicated to comments.

It contains all the useful settings for the management of discussion options on our blog.

There are many options on this page and they are well documented. So, in these pages we will list only:

- options for the notification of the contents to and from the other blogs (in particular useful for management of pingback);
- options for managing comments (useful to decide whether comments should be free or put into moderation queue and, also, requirements for commenting);
- options for email notification of comments;
- greylist concerning comments with specific keywords, that must be into moderation queue;
- blacklists for comments containing specific keywords, not to approve;
- options for managing and displaying avatars for users who write comments, using the comment system.

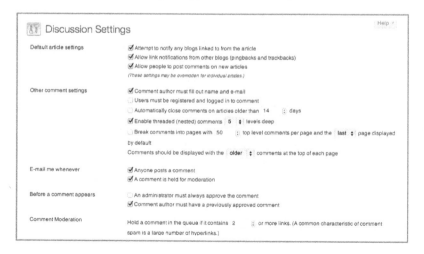

Media

The settings concerning media are used to manage various aspects and, in particular:

- the default and maximum size of the images included in posts and pages;
- the ability to embed multimedia content such as videos from YouTube or links about services as Flickr;
- the path to use to store files uploaded and inserted into posts and pages (default path: wp-content/uploads).

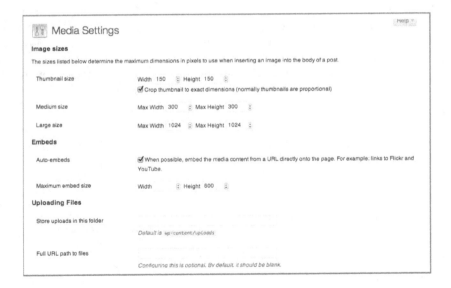

Privacy

The section on privacy settings allows to inhibit access to our blog by search engine's crawlers.

In particular, this option turns on the "robots" meta tag in each page of the blog (<meta name="robots" content="noindex, nofollow">), to indicate the crawlers on various search engines must not consider the blog, during their indexing activities.

Permalinks

This section allows us to configure the permalinks of the blog.

A permalink is a kind of URL that refers to a particular web page where the contents are implemented with the intention of not change for long periods of time. Not surprisingly, the term permalink arises from a contraction of two words: "permanent" and "link".

In this section, we can decide how to represent the blog permalinks.

In particular, we can determine the structure of links that we intend to use in the blog.

To better understand the permalinks, let's make an example.

During Chapter 5, we saw how to create a post. By default, the URL directed to this post of WordPress is represented in this way: http://mybook.space4tutorial.com/?p=12, where the number 12 represents the id of the post as inserted within database.

If, within the permalink configuration page, we configure the option "Day and name", we can use a different and more mnemonic system of links to list our posts. More precisely, the posts may also be referenced using the following permanent link: http:// mybook.space4tutorial.com/2012/08/09/test-post-no-1/.

This feature is very useful from the point of view of indexing by search engines, because if we insert into the title a certain keyword, it will also be included in the permalink, with consequent benefits in terms of optimization SEO.

Chapter 13 - The "secrets" of a successful blog

How to make your blog interesting

In previous chapters we covered the various aspects of running a blog, especially from the technical and practical point of view, starting from creation and continuing through development of web content and use of the various additional features, up to the user management.

Of course, as already stated in the introduction, this book does not pretend to be the definitive guide to WordPress, but wants to give an overall description of everything that concerns the management of a blog using this wonderful CMS. It's clear that, even if this book is primarily related to the realization of a blog made with WordPress, in these pages there are useful information even for those who should decide to adopt different platforms for blogging, in the future.

In particular, in this and in following chapters, we will discuss various topics related to managing a blog, which are independent of platform chosen and that can clearly decree the greater or lesser success of our blog.

Before going ahead with the discussion, however, let me say once a very important thing: achieve the success of a blog is not easy, as many readers may think.

In this sense, you can find on the Internet, every day, thousands and thousands of websites where there are promises to reveal the secrets to get a successful blog. So, many readers believe that it is enough to know a few "special" tricks to increase the number of visitors, suddenly and without effort.

Oh yes, because the main element of satisfaction, taken as a reference by most webmasters and more precisely by bloggers, is the number of requests received monthly or daily.

Based on this conviction many companies arose, both nationally and internationally, whose principal activity is the provision of courses and the sale of so-called "information products". Some of them provide services and information material which I consider high quality (ebooks, video courses, reports, etc.), while others are unfortunately limited to gathering and reporting news and information of common use and delivers them as a sort of "magic potion" for success, often at considerable prices.

My personal opinion is that, most of the time, nothing is better than learning the personally experienced lessons!

Personally, I do not hide that I purchased several information products and found, along with useful information, a lot of "junk". However, I think this helped me to understand that, in addition to people who do their work very seriously, there are others who take advantage of the enthusiasm of a blogger who would like to see its own blog not only visited by its friends, but also by other persons.

I'm saying this because I am firmly convinced that, as with any other activity, to ensure that your blog has the expected success, you need commitment and dedication.

In other words, setting up a blog and inserting two advertising banners and then turning off your computer and laze, in the expectation that it will produce "revenue up to 4 zeroes" (as stated by some slogans, on the Internet), is not enough!

That said, let's see what are the secrets to get a successful blog, especially if it is just born and it's still unknown to everyone.

Of course, these are neither secret nor tricks that work 100% for any type of blog you want to create, but simple tips and suggestions arising from the practical and personal experience.

The first among the suggestions is to make our own blog interesting.

How can we do it? Before, creating interesting content!

In this context, the choice of right "niche" is critical and of fundamental importance. And the considerations can be many and different from each other.

In fact, for example, we might consider that an area like information technology may be too competitive for our tastes, because there are many blogs that cover topics related to the world of computers, cell phones and smartphones, and so on.

As well, between a blog about computers and another one concerning food, we might consider that the latter has a minor number of users, but very "loyal", so we just have to "introduce" our blog to readers, and conquer them.

Still, we might prefer to make a blog about television and, in particular, concerning the gossip, rather than create a blog on classical music, because it could be indirectly "driven" by some television programs with greater force than what we might unleash being alone.

However, in spite of the arguments that we decide to treat, our blog should be interesting, at least for the audience of users that we have chosen.

To implement this, our blog must have content that may correspond to the needs and requests of users. In practice, we should follow one of the fundamental rules of the perfect trader: "let feel the need to the customer and give him what he want!".

To do this, we must ensure that the user access our blog, and then find the content useful to its purposes.

Eventually, it can be useful, before the design phase of the blog, to figure out what might be the needs of our target users, possibly by conducting surveys and market researches.

Obviously, the concept of "interesting" can vary from person to person, in relation to the topics discussed. In fact, a specific post written and published on our blog will not be necessarily considered as "interesting" by all readers.

Choosing the right "niche" allows us to focus on a particular type of content and even the reader who is not interested in a single post could recognize in our blog a valuable reference point.

For example, on a blog that covers astronomy, we can find posts about the solar system, as well as posts about quasars and theories that govern the Universe. Not all readers are fascinated by string theory, concerning the birth of the Universe, but some of them, of course, finding also other interesting posts (for example, regarding nebulae), will certainly come back to visit, or will add the blog to the list of his bookmarks.

Choice of content

To make a blog really interesting, we must, without doubt, write high quality posts.

For quality posts we do not necessarily intend to very long pages.

Rather, we intend to posts dealing certain topics in a comprehensive manner, presented in a "professional" writing style, correctly spelled, with no grammatical errors and a language more fluid and light as possible, which makes the reading restful to the user.

To write quality content, you need to know the topics and know them well. This, not only to avoid the risk of mistakes, but also because if we want a successful blog, we must also be able to deal with various requests for assistance and support that come from readers, through the comment system.

The success of a blog and the interest in it are directly proportional to the participation of users and, if they leave comments, we must answer them in a precise manner, in accordance with any represented problems.

In addition to the quality of the posts, quantity is very important. That does not mean that we have to write 40 posts a day, without pause.

Rather, it's better to write a good quality post a week.

Many bloggers often start with a blog full of posts, churning out new posts at the rate of 10 per day and then, after a few months, they end up discouraged and give up the blog himself, tired of updating.

Not to mention that, sometimes, if we publish 10 posts a day without interruption, we may not develop adequately good quality content.

For the realization of good posts, we must avoid the "cut and paste" from other websites. Inspiration from other sites is acceptable and often leads to address the same topic from different perspectives, but we should always make adequate preparation and depth of content.

Furthermore, our blog should not only address matters of interest to us, but especially those topics interesting and useful from the point of view of our readers.

And it should, if possible, include information not available on other websites.

Only in this way the users will appreciate our work and come back on our blog, with interest and pleasure.

Choosing an attractive theme

Of course, the content is not the only thing to watch out for having a successful blog. In fact, our blog can be the best in terms of written posts, but if it has not a catchy graphics, it can not be evaluated fairly.

We have already described how to find and install themes for WordPress.

Here, we must say that a theme should be chosen and possibly customized in relation to the discussed topics.

For example, a theme with a background full of flowers, do not mesh very well with a blog that deals with economics and finance. Similarly, on a cooking blog is difficult to match some buttons with a "techno" style. While, on the contrary, we can bind a theme with many flowers to a food blog, or with a blog about gardening.

Another thing to keep in mind when we choose a theme and, then, when we write new posts, is the graphical layout.

In particular, the arrangement of images and of text can make reading the blog content more or less comfortable and relaxing. The correct placement of ads banners, moreover, can make reading easier, improving the so-called "experience" of the user. In fact, it will be more inclined to visit our blog.

Another important element, especially if we are interested in a target group of users from a particular country, is the fact of having a localized theme, translated into the language of our type of potential visitors.

For example, if our blog is intended for italian users, we can install a theme with italian localization (or, if we have some experience about PHP, we can directly modify template, by adding italian localization, by using the specific editor, as discussed in Chapter 8).

If we want to write posts for users coming from more Countries, we can also decide to create a multilingual blog, by installing and activating some translation plugins, or by directly translating content of our blog.

As you can see, there are many solutions and the goal is to make our visitors feel at their ease as possible.

Writing for web

Writing for the blog is not always easy. We have to know the topics, choose images and other multimedia material useful for better representation of what we write and, especially, we must adopt a set of stylistic rules, specific of web writing.

For example, the approach used to write the text of a brochure for the promotion of a product is not the same as that used when writing the text of a technical report.

And it could not be the same, since the purpose is different.

In fact, the text of a brochure is aimed at stimulating the interest of potential buyers in a product, and must have certain characteristics, while that of a technical report is to describe in detail a topic and, therefore, must present a form of quite different.

Similarly, writing text for a blog and, more generally, for a website, we must use a specific style, able to involve users and lead to so-called "conversion", that is their interest in our posts.

When writing content for a blog, we must follow these rules:

- **<u>Write using simple language</u>**

When we create a blog, generally, we assume that someone will read it. Based on covered topics and on the type of users who read our content, we must strive to write as simple and understandable as possible.

This, of course, does not mean trivial. Rather, it means that we must write legibly, using a language that is not necessarily polished and full of unusual linguistic expressions, but concise and clear, if necessary, describing the concepts that may seem obvious, acronyms and jargon that could create difficult for readers.

In this way, the reading will be fluid and users will be able to assess positively our content.

- **Use as much text as necessary**

This obviously does not means that we must count, one by one, the words to use when writing a post. Instead, it means writing our own posts keeping in mind that a short post is not synonym of poor quality, and that a very long post is not always a very good post.

The rule to remember is: write the right amount of text you need to address the topic, without writing more or less.

- **Do not twist too much about the concepts to be treated**

The key word is "relevance". Given a specific topic, we must not turn around the concepts, but write down everything that we believe relevant, and avoid giving the impression of wanting to "stretch the soup", especially when this is not necessary.

- **Immediately expose the main concepts**

Return the key concepts from the first rows of text and also of each single paragraph. In this way, we simplify a lot reading and we allow the user to find out whether a post is interesting, or not.

This is also because user that is reading a blog does not have the same attitude of the reader of a book. He is not necessarily cutting out a space to be dedicated to his relax but, instead, he is often driven by the frenzy to get the information he need, as soon as possible.

Therefore, a post where users do not understand the concepts discussed immediately is discarded.

- **Addressing topics comprehensively**

If we want our items are considered useful and that our blog is worthy to be visited, we must try to treat each specific topic in a correct and complete manner. Everything, always with a clear and concise language.

- **Write brilliantly**

It is important to write in order to represent the concepts in a brilliant way, not in the sense to treat them with humor, but rather to expose them in the direction of a fluid language and showing also the practical aspects. This, in order to "tickle" the reader and "keep careful" him about what we are writing.

Choosing the right font

Also the use of a specific font, rather than another, can affect the player and the success of the blog.

Moreover, the appropriate use of italics, bold, underline, as well as alignment and tabulation, can encourage or not the user in reading the content.

For example, highlight the key concepts or key phrases, using bold, can be successful, compared with creation of a post without any formatting.

Similarly, the use of a bulleted (not ordered) or numbered list, to describe a set of elements, is certainly more appropriate, compared with some elements that are just separated by commas.

Still, writing posts separating different blocks of text can greatly facilitate its understanding.

With regard to colors, we should prefer, over light backgrounds, not too bright characters and saturated colors, while on dark backgrounds, light colored characters, not too similar to the background color.

Regarding the links, we should avoid the same color used for not linked text.

These are general guidelines that may apply to the web, but at the same time they are useful for other forms of communication.

Choosing the best title

The title is the first thing we read in a page or a post.

Therefore, we should understand what is the rest of the text, simply by reading the title.

If the user doesn't clearly understand the topic of the post, how can we think to convince him to read it?

For this reason, we must include within each post title the indication about topics addressed, in the manner as complete as possible.

Because this is the only way to attract the user, right from the start. And the user's impression will decide the success or failure of our work as bloggers.

Moreover, the title should be concise. In several cases, three or four words are enough to describe very complex posts, while in other circumstances we should be more verbose. But, we should always try to "send out the message" of what user will find in our post.

In this way, from the psychological point of view, the user will start with "the right foot" and, if interested in the topics, he will read our post to the end.

But what can we do in practice to obtain good title for our posts?

Here is some information that may be helpful:
- Prefer short titles, but at the same time descriptive;
- If possible, avoid abbreviations; an expression that was particularly impressed on my mind, during a training course, is "synthesize, do not abbreviate";
- Enter in the title, one or more words considered "key";
- Avoid generic titles such as "Post 1" (in this book, we created a post titled "Test Post no. 1" but, of course, this title was used only as a demonstrative example);
- Create original and unique titles, to stimulate the readers' attention.

Using social networks

A successful blog bases its strength on the use of all the available promotion channels.

In this sense, we must say that, especially in recent years, the popularity of social networks has added new ways to publicize a blog to the greatest number of users.

These methods, of course, are in addition to other forms of promotion existing previously and they are, very often, more effective, compared with normal advertising obtained by the most common circuits available on the Internet.

Furthermore, it is important to know that advertising obtained through the use of social networks is easy and free, unlike the traditional kind, often very expensive.

This is the reason why many blogs are also connected to a Facebook page, or to a Twitter profile or, more frequently, to both the social networks, and in addition their owners are online with professional profiles of LinkedIn and other social channels.

The advantage offered by social networks derives from the fact that, for their intrinsic characteristics, this kind of internet service involves the participation of a large number of users, who primarily produce content.

It is estimated that social networks involve more than 80% of all Internet users at a global level.

Since social networks base their operation and success on the fact that users are content creators themselves, a good way to promote our blog might be represented by the fact to ensure that users themselves write about us on one or more social networks.

How can we talk about our blog on social networks like Facebook and / or Twitter (just to mention the most important ones)?

Here are some methods:

- Using "social sharing" buttons

These are buttons that allow users who find our posts interesting and worthy of attention to share links to related pages on their own Facebook wall, Twitter profile, and so on.

If user A shares a link to our post on our profile, all friends of him can view what in the jargon of the social network is called "update status". And, if they click on the shared link, they will reach the post shared by user A.

The use of these buttons can be very useful, especially when blogger is able to develop a good "virality", that is to say a good diffusion capacity of its posts, by this mechanism, very similar to a "by word of mouth".

The addition of these buttons to our blog can be performed using special plugins or, very often, it can be included among the features provided by the chosen theme.

To install one of them without much effort, we just follow the steps in the appropriate chapter on plugins, for the search and installation.

Personally, what I use most often for this purpose is "Add to Any: Share / Bookmark / Email Buttons", but only in WordPress repository we can find many other plugins that perform the same tasks.

- Using systems as "Like" button, "ReTweet" e "+1"

During 2011, Google has definitely come into the world of social networks, with its system of "+1", "g+", or Google Plus, which allows a user to specify a particular content as useful and / or interesting.

Prior to Google, Facebook already used a similar system that allowed users to indicate their interest about a given post or web page: the "like" button.

The same thing with regard to Twitter, that with special "ReTweet" buttons allows any user to report, to those who follow its own profile (followers), the links to content considered useful and interesting.

The addition of the "like" or "+1" button allows us to promote our blog in a slightly different way, compared with sharing buttons. But it has the same potential, in terms of the achieved results.

Again, to add "like" or "+1", if the theme does not already have it, we must just install a specific plugin, performing the usual procedure concerning the search and installation it, described in Chapter 10.

- Creating a Facebook page

The creation of a Facebook page can help in promoting the blog more than you think, because it allows the sending of updates to "fans" in a simple and effective.

However, bloggers are often discouraged by the effort required for populating the page itself (increasing the number of fans participating in our page), especially in the early stages.

So, my personal suggestion is to make also a worthwhile Facebook page, providing useful information and other content that may be of interest to users, who will not hesitate to become fans.

Commenting on other blogs

What is the best way to introduce your blog? For many bloggers, one of the best methods is to comment on other blogs.

In fact, commenting on other blogs that deal with similar themes of ours can become one of the most effective ways to promote the blog, in an indirect way, especially in the beginning.

This is because most blogging platforms, including WordPress, provide the opportunity to indicate, together with our comments, a link to a website.

However, to comment does not mean to SPAM!

In fact, there are different ways to comment, and certainly leaving unnecessary comments like "nice post", "great site" and similar, is not the best.

Ideal is to leave comments on other blogs regarding the same topics of ours, making it clear that our actions spring from the real interest and not arise from the desire to spread our link in the world.

Possibly, if we know the topics very well, we can also comment adding more information than what is already written by other bloggers, in order to enrich any discussion and gain the respect and attention of those who follow other bloggers and that can find in us one of the possible reference points.

Chapter 14 - Tools for webmasters

The presence on search engines

One of the most fascinating things, in relation to the implementation and subsequent management of a blog, is the awareness that, when we write posts or other types of web content, they can be read by many people, who can express their opinion, compare them with our own ideas and, more generally, participate in our blog.

However, we have already said that to get a participated blog we should strive to increase gradually our users and, to achieve this goal, presence of our blog in the major search engines becomes decisive.

What does it means?

It means, essentially, giving users the ability to surf the Internet to find out our blog using one or more keywords in their searches.

The majority of users, or better, all of them, beyond their usual websites, does not know and could not know the web addresses for all the sites available on the Internet.

Therefore, a user who searches information on the Internet, usually uses one or more search engines and reaches the contents of interest by querying these motors with one or more words, in relation to the topics of interest.

The most important search engine at present is certainly Google (http://www.google.com) and appears to its users with a screen like the following:

This is not the only search engine, there are many others, such as Bing, although I think its supremacy over others is well known to everyone.

If our blog is among the Google results, we can trust without any effort on a good number of visits. Generally, a search engine like Google is able to carry up to 60 - 70% more visits to our blog. But we need to be seen by its crawler, by its "engine" software, that scans all (or most) websites that appear to the world.

So, we must take all appropriate measures to improve its presence among the search results for certain keywords.

In Chapter 12, within the paragraph dedicated to the WordPress settings, we saw an option on the "Privacy" blog. This option, as already explained, is used to allow or deny the scan of the blog by the major search engines. Except in some cases, this option should always be configured to allow scanning. Otherwise, the risk is to make a blog completely inaccessible to search engines and, therefore, cutting it off from the results that users can find in their own searches.

There are many things we can do to improve our blog's presence on search engines. In particular, we can optimize it by using SEO techniques.

SEO stands for Search Engine Optimization and consists of all those activities aimed at improving the presence of a website on search engines, with the goal of increasing the volume of users coming from searches made on the Internet.

These activities include both the optimization performed on the HTML pages of the blog, and those that are made working on the web content (posts and so on).

Aspects concerning the optimization SEO are too many and a book of 100 more pages would not be enough to expose all of them.

Moreover, they are continuously changing, because search engines are constantly updated to improve the quality of returned results and to give, to the user performing the search, all web content that may interest him more and / or be more useful for him.

For this reason, even reading a book that deals specifically with SEO techniques, alone, may not be sufficient, especially if you want to get the most from search engines, for your blog.

Regarding Google, on the Italian official blog set up by the Colossus of Mountain View (reached at the link http://googleitalia.blogspot.com), a few weeks ago the new edition of "Google optimization for search engines" was introduced. This edition was born because of the need to provide an additional tool for webmasters who want to improve their presence on Google, and it contains much information that may be useful also against other search engines.

So, my personal recommendation is to download the PDF version, available in Italian at the following link: http://www.google.com/intl/it/webmasters/docs/search-engine-optimization-starter-guide-it.pdf e in English at link http://static.googleusercontent.com/external_content/untrusted_dlcp/www.google.com/en//webmasters/docs/search-engine-optimization-starter-guide.pdf.

However, in these pages are summarized some of the "cornerstone" rules of the optimization SEO:

- Put the most important content at the top of pages and / or posts. To do this, referring to WordPress, you should prefer the themes with a layout that puts the text of the posts in the top left;
- Use format settings of text in a manner that is functional to the content, with particular reference to the semantics, for example highlighting concepts and keywords with bold,

dividing paragraphs, using lists and other elements in a "reasonable" manner with exposed concepts;

- Distinguishing titles and subtitles from the rest of the text;
- Prefer the use of standard HTML code, compared to JavaScript, to manage menus;
- With specific reference to WordPress, prefer descriptive permalinks, containing within themselves the titles of posts, rather than the id. The latter is the default configuration of WordPress, but within the menu "Settings" → "Permalink" you can edit it to make sure that the URL of posts contains also titles;
- Use one or more Sitemaps for indicating URLs (to the engines) to be considered in the search, and possibly the priority with which they must be updated.

XML sitemaps

XML sitemaps are one of the mechanisms most often overlooked by some bloggers and webmasters, that may make the difference between a blog and others.

An XML sitemap is simply an XML file containing a list of links, corresponding, in the case of a WordPress blog, to all the posts, all the pages of type "archive", all pages that contain posts written by a specific user, home page, etc..

What for? To communicate to search engines which are the pages that we want to scan. In practice, it is as an index of the blog, which allows us very easy to tell search engines what are pages of our blog (or, more generally, our website) that we want to be read by the crawler and shown in search results.

The currently used standard was originally introduced by Google, but it has also been adopted by other search engines, like Yahoo and Bing, thanks to a special type of license (Attribution/ Share Alike Creative Commons License).

At the time of writing these pages, trying to open the XML sitemap of my blog SPACE 4 TUTORIAL via the Safari browser, I can see the following content:

XML Sitemap

This is a XML Sitemap which is supposed to be processed by search engines like Google, MSN Search and YAHOO.

It was generated using the Blogging-Software WordPress and the Google Sitemap Generator Plugin by Arne Brachhold.

You can find more information about XML sitemaps on sitemaps.org and Google's list of sitemap programs.

URL	Priority	Change Frequency	LastChange (GMT)
http://www.space4tutorial.com/	100%	Daily	2011-11-08 00:21
http://www.space4tutorial.com/2011/11/08/partypoker-it-e-il-poker-online-e-servito/	20%	Monthly	2011-11-08 00:21
http://www.space4tutorial.com/lo-staff/	60%	Weekly	2011-09-20 07:31
http://www.space4tutorial.com/2011/08/13/real-drums-per-mac-video-di-closer-to-the-edge/	20%	Monthly	2011-08-13 09:43
http://www.space4tutorial.com/2011/06/16/real-drums-per-iphone-ecco-a-voi-la-nuova-versione-4-0/	20%	Monthly	2011-06-15 22:56
http://www.space4tutorial.com/2009/02/06/interest-calculator-unapplicazione-iphone-per-il-calcolo-degli-interessi-disponibile-sullapp-store/	20%	Monthly	2011-04-16 13:24
http://www.space4tutorial.com/2009/02/21/real-drums-trasforma-il-tuo-iphone-ipod-touch-in-una-batteria-musicale/	20%	Monthly	2011-04-16 13:24
http://www.space4tutorial.com/2009/11/22/interest-calculator-per-iphone-si-aggiorna/	20%	Monthly	2011-04-16 13:24
http://www.space4tutorial.com/2010/04/11/real-drums-suonare-gli-u2-con-liphone/	20%	Monthly	2011-04-16 13:20

As we can see from this screenshot, via a XML sitemap is also possible to give a rough indication, to one or more search engines, about the update frequency of pages ("Priority" column), as well as notify them about new content, so they can be updated by the search engines within a few hours.

This is also a screenshot of how the XML code appears, about a typical XML sitemap:

```
<?xml version="1.0" encoding="UTF-8"?><?xml-stylesheet type="text/xsl" href="http://
    www.space4tutorial.com/wp-content/plugins/google-sitemap-generator/sitemap.xsl"?><!--
    generator="wordpress/3.2.1" -->
<!-- sitemap-generator-url="http://www.arnebrachhold.de" sitemap-generator-version="3.2.6" -->
<!-- generated-on="8 November 2011 00:22" -->
<urlset xmlns:xsi="http://www.w3.org/2001/XMLSchema-instance" xsi:schemaLocation="http://
    www.sitemaps.org/schemas/sitemap/0.9 http://www.sitemaps.org/schemas/sitemap/0.9/sitemap.xsd"
    xmlns="http://www.sitemaps.org/schemas/sitemap/0.9">   <url>
        <loc>http://www.space4tutorial.com/</loc>
        <lastmod>2011-11-08T00:21:40+00:00</lastmod>
        <changefreq>daily</changefreq>
        <priority>1.0</priority>
    </url>
    <url>
        <loc>http://www.space4tutorial.com/2011/11/08/partypoker-it-e-il-poker-online-e-servito/</
            loc>
        <lastmod>2011-11-08T00:21:40+00:00</lastmod>
        <changefreq>monthly</changefreq>
        <priority>0.2</priority>
    </url>
    <url>
        <loc>http://www.space4tutorial.com/lo-staff/</loc>
        <lastmod>2011-09-20T07:31:24+00:00</lastmod>
        <changefreq>weekly</changefreq>
        <priority>0.6</priority>
    </url>
    <url>
        <loc>http://www.space4tutorial.com/2011/08/13/real-drums-per-mac-video-di-closer-to-the-
            edge/</loc>
        <lastmod>2011-08-13T09:43:28+00:00</lastmod>
        <changefreq>monthly</changefreq>
        <priority>0.2</priority>
    </url>
    <url>
        <loc>http://www.space4tutorial.com/2011/06/16/real-drums-per-iphone-ecco-a-voi-la-nuova-
            versione-4-0/</loc>
        <lastmod>2011-06-15T22:56:46+00:00</lastmod>
        <changefreq>monthly</changefreq>
        <priority>0.2</priority>
    </url>
    <url>
        <loc>http://www.space4tutorial.com/2009/02/06/interest-calculator-unapplicazione-iphone-per-
            il-calcolo-degli-interessi-disponibile-sullapp-store/</loc>
        <lastmod>2011-04-16T13:24:37+00:00</lastmod>
        <changefreq>monthly</changefreq>
        <priority>0.2</priority>
    </url>
    <url>
        <loc>http://www.space4tutorial.com/2009/02/21/real-drums-trasforma-il-tuo-iphone-ipod-touch-
```

Among the huge amount of plugins available in the official repository of WordPress, there are several of them dedicated to the production of XML sitemaps.

These plugins can be installed and used in our blog via the simple procedure already described in Chapter 10, concerning WordPress plugins.

Among the different plugins concerning the management of XML sitemaps, I can indicate "Google XML Sitemaps", a plugin that I used on several occasions for different blogs. It allows to create a sitemap configuring different aspects, and to ensure the notification of its updates to various search engines.

To submit one or more sitemaps to the major search engines, can be extremely useful to use online tools for webmasters, provided by the search engines themselves.

In particular, Google offers users the "Google Webmasters Tools" (located at https://www.google.com/webmasters/tools/), which in addition to sending XML sitemaps, provides a range of software tools to periodically check the "health" of a website.

A similar system, developed by Microsoft for the Bing search engine, is available at the link http://www.bing.com/toolbox/webmaster/.

Besides these tools, many other services are available online, free and paid, which enables creation, validation and transmission to the search engines of XML sitemaps. Simply make a simple search, using your preferred engine, to obtain a good list of such services.

Google Webmasters Tools

Google Webmasters Tools is a collection of useful services available to webmasters to improve the visibility of our website, with reference to the most important search engine: Google, precisely.

As we already said, they allow, in addition to the simple transmission of XML sitemaps, to constantly check the health of our blog (or website in general), allowing us to know what are the searches that led users to visit it, the number of links to it, the keywords that generated more visits, etc..

The use of the Google Webmasters Tools is free, but we must have an account, or we must create a new one for the occasion. Here is a screenshot that shows the dashboard related to my blog TRAVAGLIANTE.COM (http://www.travagliante.com):

Some of the information provided by Webmasters Tools are very useful. For example, we can understand what are the most searched terms by users, or what are words that have brought visitors to our blog. In practice, we can focus our attention on user behavior and we can evaluate all search query for which we would like to enhance the competitiveness between the results shown by search engines.

Taking a look at the menu "Traffic" → "Search Queries", for example, we can get a page containing the main search queries that routed users on the blog.

For my blog SPACE 4 TUTORIAL, I noted that the search query that took more impressions (page views) is "images for facebook". In addition, one of the keywords that brought more visits is "iphone".

So, since the blog SPACE 4 TUTORIAL concerns mainly computer and Internet, I might think to increase traffic by simply writing a few posts about Facebook or Apple iPhone. And, effectively, by using other online tools available on the Internet, it is possible to know what are the words that users search more frequently on Google and other search engines, for all subject areas and I can say with certainty that "Facebook" is one of the most searched words, about computer and Internet.

It also very useful to know if there are errors during the scan of the links of our blog, revealed by the "crawlers" of their search engines (in this case, specifically by the Google crawler).

For this reason, Google Webmasters Tools also allow us to know what are the links that generated error 404 (page not found), error 300 (redirection error), or other problems that prevented their web content scanning.

Below is a screenshot concerning errors that occurred in my personal blog, during the last 3 months:

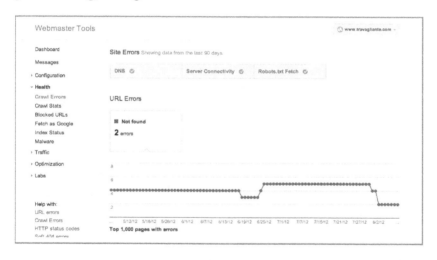

And here there are the main links that generated a 404 code, which corresponds to "page not found":

	Priority ▾	URL	Response Code	Detected
☐	1	2012/06/wordpress-dalla-a-alla-w-adesso-anche-su-lafeltrinelli-it/feed/	404	6/23/12
☐	2	2012/06/wordpress-dalla-a-alla-w-adesso-anche-su-lafeltrinelli-it/	404	7/27/12
				1-2 of 2 ⟨ ⟩

In addition to this diagnostic information, Webmasters Tools allow you to also check the status of the scan performed by the Google crawler, along with some important statistics such as number of pages scanned daily, downloaded kilobytes and the minimum, maximum and average download time for pages of the website.

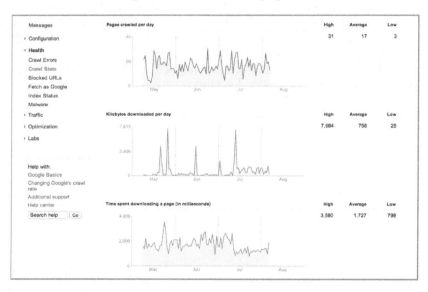

In particular, an aspect to which Google shows great attention and for which these tools can be useful is the load speed of a website.

In fact, since the last quarter of 2010, Google has introduced some changes to its own algorithms for the evaluation of websites that reward sites that load pages faster and, conversely, penalize those sites characterized by very slowly. These changes stemmed from the assumption that if the user accesses a slow website, he tends to leave it, because he can't get web content.

For this reason, today we can not neglect this important aspect, which can be identified and measured indirectly by using the tools available in Webmasters Tools.

Besides these tools, Google Webmasters Tools allow us to get suggestions about optimizing our website's HTML code, especially regarding the presence of duplicate meta descriptions, too long or too short, missing or duplicate title tags, etc..

As for the XML sitemaps, Google Webmasters Tools allow us to manage the XML files containing the list of links and to be informed of any indexing problems.

The screen concerning the management of sitemaps, looks like this:

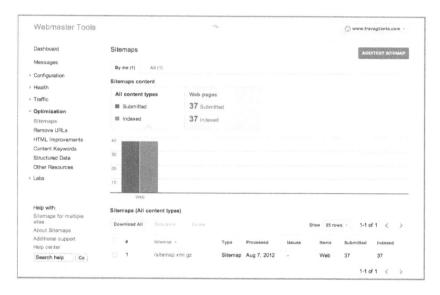

As we can see, through this page we can also check the number of indexed URLs, in relation to those sent via the sitemap.

The Google Webmaster Tools have several benefits, in addition to those described, but listing all of them is beyond the scope of this book.

For this reason, for a complete description of the functionality of this important instrument, please refer to its online guide, made available directly from Google Webmasters Tools and searchable within the same.

Bing Webmasters Tools

As already mentioned, Bing also offers some handy tools for webmasters, for free.

Here is the main page of Bing Webmasters Tools:

Many of its tools perform the same functions which we already found in the Google Webmasters Tools. So, why use this service? Well, because registration of our website to Bing Webmaster Tools allows us to bring up it even on the search engine signed by Microsoft. Therefore, why should we deprive ourselves of visits that are generated also by this search engine?

So my personal suggestion is to register our websites on both tools, along with respective XML sitemaps. In this way, we can take advantage of the benefits of both.

Also, signing up for this online service can be useful to appear on other search engines and directories, such as "Yahoo! Search", which has consented to the absorption of its software product called "Site Explorer" directly inside of Bing Webmaster Tools, as we can read on the link http://siteexplorer.search.yahoo.com/index.php:

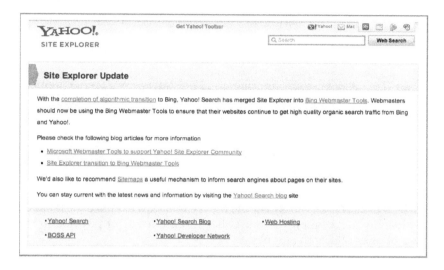

Also for the use of several features of Bing Webmaster Tools, we can refer to online documentation accessible from the pages of the service itself.

Tools for statistics

While maintaining a blog, besides the use of tools for webmasters already seen, tools for acquisition and management of website's statistics are certainly useful and necessary.

These tools can help us understand all the different aspects of the requests received from our blogs (or, more generally, from our website).

In particular, most of the tools available for free on the Internet is able to carry out the monitoring of users, with particular reference to the following types of information:

- Number of page views;
- Number of unique visitors;
- Content of the website that is visited with the greatest frequency;

- Provenance, from the geographical point of view, of our visitors;
- Average duration of visits, registered on the website;
- Main sources of our traffic.

The use of a monitoring tool on our website is extremely important, because it may assist us in the understanding of user behavior, in relation to content available in our blog.

For example, it can make us understand what are the most popular posts or categories of our website, what content they want to read (posts that involve the largest number of users) and, consequently, on what topics we must focus our attention when we create new posts and more generally, new web content.

Furthermore, analysis of the search keywords can help us evaluate which of them we must "bet", to improve our position in the result pages of search engines.

These tools, finally, beyond any possible assessment (especially regarding the SEO optimization), can enable us to obtain a "feedback" for the work done to create our website and let us know if we are going in the right direction, or not.

In fact, by using them, a blogger (or webmaster) can also know the degree of appreciation that people show towards the blog (or site), just reading some parameters, such as the average number of page views per each visitor.

The free online tools that allow management of user statistics, are many and different. Among the most common, we can mention:

- Google Analytics (http://www.google.com/analytics/);
- HiStats (http://www.histats.com/);
- ShinyStat (http://www.shinystat.com/).

Personally, the one I use most often is Google Analytics, because I can access it using the same account of electronic mail GMail, and Google Webmasters Tools.

However, since the basic information provided by these web services is more or less the same, I would not recommend one of them, at the expense of others.

Therefore, the choice is yours, even after you have tried all of them (one at a time, of course).

For example, here is how a Histats typical dashboard appears (taken from the live demo, available on its website):

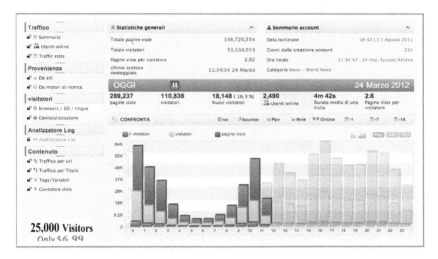

How we can see, looking at the side menu items, represented information let us know the statistics about visits, classified according to source of traffic, geographic location, type of browsers and operating system, language and content displayed.

In addition, information is given on the pages visited, unique visitors, pages visited by each visitor and average duration of each visit.

ShinyStat provides similar information, and it is another service available both free of charge (ShinyStat Free), and with paid options (Pro, Business and ISPs). It is dedicated, as Histats, to the monitoring of users of a website:

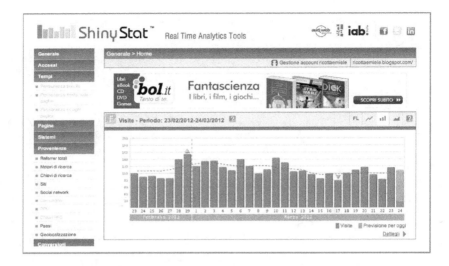

As for the Webmasters Tools, for a complete description of all the features of these services, please see the related documentation, available as online help, for each of them.

Same, regarding installation and verification of the respective "tracking codes", those codes (consisting of a mix of HTML, PHP and JavaScript) that must be installed on the website for the proper functioning of these tools.

Google Analytics

Among the tools needed to get statistics about the visits of our own blog or, more generally, of our website, we must mention Google Analytics.

Google Analytics is a free monitoring service, useful to get detailed statistical analysis of users. At the moment, it is the most used on the web, as other services powered by Google.

Here is how its main screen appears, relative to a blog that I created with no great pretensions, and launched a few weeks ago for a friend of mine.

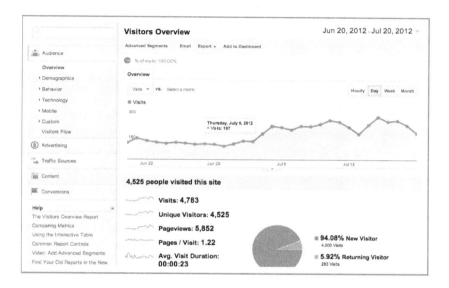

As we can see, ultimately, the information provided is more or less always the same. In particular, it includes:

- the total number of visits, in the time interval defined by the user;
- the number of unique visitors;
- page views;
- average page views for each visitor;
- an indication, in percentage, relative to new visitors.

In addition, Google Analytics provides the following important information:

- the average duration of each visit;

- bounce rate (this is an indication whose importance is often underestimated. In fact, it describes, with a percentage, how often a user access the website and leaves it, because he is not interested. It is useful to understand, on average, the degree of appreciation of our blog / site. It should be as low as possible);
- the language of the visitors;
- geographical origin, with an indication of the Countries and towns where the traffic is generated;
- the browser used, the operating system, and service provider of connectivity used by visitors;
- the resolution of the screen used, in the case where visitors are browsing by a mobile device (for example, smartphones, or tablets);
- the source of visits, divided by visits from search engines, links from other web sites, direct traffic, or from advertising campaigns (such as those provided by AdWords);
- The most used keywords to reach our site;
- the contents displayed, along with the number of obtained page views, in absolute value and as a percentage;
- pages of incoming and outgoing from the website;
- speed of website.

In addition to those listed, there is a range of additional information that can be achieved by connecting Google Webmaster Tools, Google Analytics, Google AdWords (tool for enabling advertising to pay) and Google AdSense (for the monetization of websites, in practice the normal complement of AdWords).

A very special feature of Google Analytics is the "Visitors Flow", which gives us an idea of the steps followed by users while browsing our website:

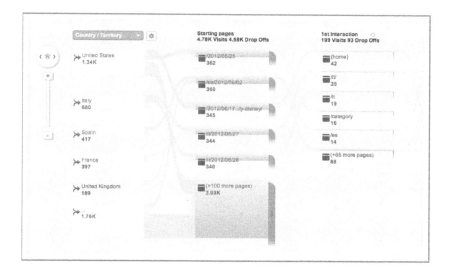

Through features such as this, Google Analytics allows us to study in detail the behavior of users, leaving nothing to the case when we want to get the most from our website.

As for other analytical tools, Google Analytics also need to install a script called "tracking code", in order to function properly.

This code contains an ID that uniquely identifies us in Google Analytics, allowing to distinguish our website from others.

Usually, the tracking code should be installed just before the closing tag </ HEAD> (for those who have no knowledge of HTML, this tag should be present on all pages of the web site).

In WordPress, the vast majority of themes, this tag is in the header.php file, editable with the PHP editor, available by clicking on "Appearance" menu, directly from the administrative panel (for more details, see Chapter 8).

We must say that, however, some themes require the installation of the Google Analytics tracking code or ID only, by using the specific options of the theme, usually available in the menu "Appearance".

Here's how the tracking code installed in one of my blog appears:

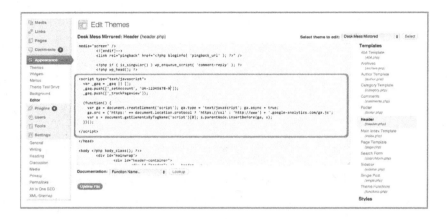

Like the two previous services, for detailed instructions for generation of the tracking code, please refer to the online documentation available on Google Analytics.

In these pages, we simply say that, to create the tracking code for our blog (http://mybook.space4tutorial.com), we must create a Google Account (if we haven't it, already) and, after logging in Google Analytics, we must select the "Admin" menu in the top bar and click on the "+ New Account" button.

On the page that appears, we must insert the requested information and accept all its terms and conditions concerning use of the service:

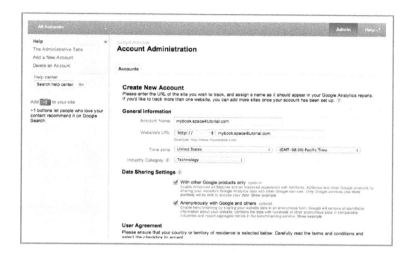

On the next page, we will see the tracking code, to be installed on the website:

Now, let's copy this code and let's access to the administrative panel of our WordPress blog (http://mybook.space4tutorial.com/wp-admin/), selecting the menu "Appearance" → "Editor".

We are entering the editor, so we must be careful. On the right side of the page that appears, there is a list of files that make up the currently active theme on the blog. Let's click on the link corresponding to the file "header.php" (Header of the blog).

Next, let's find the tag </HEAD> and, just before that, let's paste the tracking code that we copied from the web page of Google Analytics. Here's the result, as it appears on the blog http://mybook.space4tutorial.com:

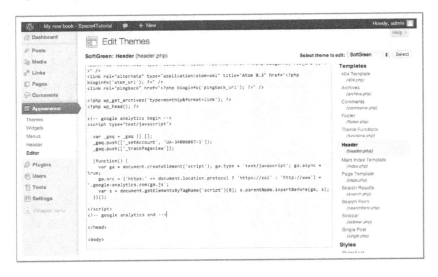

Let's click on the "Update File". From this moment, we must wait, while the script of Google Analytics collects all the statistics on users, on our own.

Information may be provided with a delay that can be up to 24 hours, but if you can't wait, you must know that the new version of Google Analytics also provides real-time consultation statistics. This feature, however, is still in beta, not definitive.

Chapter 15 - Make money with a blog

The blog as a source of income

During the previous chapters, we have analyzed most of the main aspects concerning the management of a blog, starting from its creation through the WordPress CMS, up to the analysis of visitor statistics.

Dedicating passion and commitment to maintaining a blog, we can achieve a good number of users and, at that point, we can even consider to earn money with our "online work".

If we conduct a search using Google or any other search engine, typing the words "make money with a blog", we get an infinite number of links to websites which show this or that method of earning online, through the use of a blog.

In addition, many websites promise, upon payment of an amount more or less consistently, to reveal the secrets to earn high sums of money quickly and without great effort.

Well, my personal opinion on the matter is this: without commitment and effort you can't go anywhere!

Creating a successful blog and turning it into a steady source of income is not easy, it takes dedication, time and, above all, the right idea.

The first aspect on which we must focus our attention is the kind of topics that we intend to treat. This, in fact, will determine the type of users who visit our blog and, consequently, the possibility or not to monetize through certain gain methods, rather than others.

To better describe this concept, let's resort to a practical example.

In a strictly computer, we can decide to create a blog about free software and open sources. The target users who consult this blog will typically consists of people used to look for software is available free online.

Now, bearing in mind this type of users not really used to purchase software for a fee, we must note that we can not expect to gain much by using of affiliations (affiliation method is better described in the following pages) related to computer programs. With a target of this type, pay per click campaigns (PPC) may be more effective.

Differently, with a blog concerning mainly reviews about software for Mac OS X, we can think to get higher profit margins by using affiliations related to software products. This, because people who use Apple products are more likely to buy commercial software.

Of course, the desire to earn from a blog should not be the only motivation, to establish what should be the topics to be covered in the blog.

The ideal is to talk about what we know well, regardless of income we can generate.

In fact, if we write posts about well known topics, we'll not encounter great difficulty in making the blog a reference point for visitors and we will acquire more and more users, increasing the ability to earn money.

In contrast, if we write posts about topics that don't fascinate us, after a while or at the first difficulty we will end up abandoning the blog.

On the Internet we often read about people who have managed to turn their blog into their main source of income.

Some bloggers even claim to have obtained, from their creations, substantial gains, that would amaze anyone. For example, 4 years ago, Jeremy Schoemaker (manager of the blog http://www.shoemoney.com), showed a photo with a check indicating the amount of $ 132,994.97, earned through Google AdSense.

Obviously, these are extreme cases, because earnings of this entity can be achieved only under certain circumstances.

However, the fact remains that, with a successful blog followed by many visitors, you may be able to earn very respectable amounts.

Probably, your earnings won't be your primary source of income, but they will allow you to "round up" the salary.

In this regard, it is important to consider that a blog written in English has more potential revenue, compared with a blog localized in Italian language, because it can rely on a greater number of users and, in particular, on the possibility of being visited by users coming from several countries. Ditto, for what concerns multilingual blogs.

Methods to make money with an online business are many and are based on different mechanisms.

The most common ones involve the placement of banners or text links on the blog. They are classified according to the method of remuneration:

• PPC (Pay per Click);
• CPM o CPI (Cost per Impression);
• CPA (Cost per Action).

In the following paragraphs, we will see these kind of mechanisms in more detail. In addition, we will discuss some of the most important networks that can allow us to earn money with our blogs.

Pay per Click, Cost per Impression and Cost per Action

As already mentioned, the most common methods of income through our blog consist in the exposition of a banner or text links within its web pages.

Excluding the direct sale of banners or links, typically, the involved actors are three:

• **The blogger (or, to use the most common terminology, Publisher)**
• **The operator of an ad network (or advertising network)**
• **Advertisers**

These figures interact with each other playing different roles.

Advertisers turn to the manager of advertising network, to promote their products or services. Generally, the "ad network" provides them with a software platform. This software, usually called "ad server", allows advertisers to enable or disable the advertising campaigns for their products, and to define all their characteristics.

The publisher or owner of the blog, which can be a natural person or a legal entity (a company), provides the spaces within the web pages. These spaces will be used to host the banners or links related to the ads and, by adding special scripts to the blog, he allows the ad network to publish advertise.

Finally, the manager of the advertising network, generally constituted as a company, acts as an intermediary between bloggers and advertisers, ensuring that advertisements are shown on those websites that act as publishers.

To do this, the manager of the advertising network, of course, receives money from advertisers, and it uses some to pay the webspace made available by publishers, according to terms and conditions previously agreed and accepted by them.

Payments are usually made based on three advertising models: Pay Per Click (PPC), Cost Per Impression (CPM o CPI) e Cost per Action (CPA).

With the model Pay per Click (PPC), the blogger earns for every click made by users on the links or banners. This means that, regardless of the number of times the banners or links appear on the blog, the blogger can earn only if users click on ads.

Instead, the model Cost per Impression (often abbreviated CPM or CPI) provides that the blogger earns every time the ads are displayed, regardless of whether or not users will click it. In general, the yield is indicated with reference to 1000 impressions (hence CPM = Cost Per Mille).

Finally, the model Cost per Action (CPA) provides that the blogger earns for a specific action completed by the user, such as purchasing a product, subscribing to a service, and so on. Sometimes, this method is also known as Cost Per Lead (CPL), but there is a difference: "Action" usually refers to the only activities that involve the payment of a fee (such as a purchase), while "Lead" is related to any other action which doesn't means an outflow of money for the user (for example, subscription to a newsletter).

Cost per Impression model is certainly preferred by publishers, because it does not require the active interaction of users who click on ads.

On the contrary, from the point of view of advertisers, PPC campaigns are the most productive, because on many impressions, a good part concerns users interested in the products and services advertised. Therefore, with PPC, they only pay for those clicks generated by users interested. The same goes for the CPA, by which they pay only when users perform a certain action.

For this reason, it is now rare to find an ad network entirely based on the model of advertising Cost per Impression.

In fact, the advertising channels gain much more from Pay Per Click, or a combination of PPC, CPM and CPA. In addition, the average revenue for each click or action is far greater than the revenue for each impression, just to compensate for the fact that not all impressions are generated by interested users, or more precisely, there are a few impressions made by users who are affected about products or services featured in the ads.

Internet advertising offers numerous services that provide solutions based on the three models presented, particularly on Pay Per Click.

Among the most famous networks that follow the PPC and CPM models, we mention:

- Google AdSense (http://www.google.com/adsense/);
- Heyos (http://www.heyos.com/);
- BidVertiser (http://www.bidvertiser.com/);
- Clicksor (http://www.clicksor.com/);
- HotPublisher (http://hotpublisher.org/).

To use these services, generally, a specific script must be installed in the web spaces to be allocated to advertising. This script takes care to show ads supplied by advertisers and its installation is similar to script related to statistics, discussed in the previous chapter.

Google AdSense

The most popular advertising network in the world is, without a doubt, Google AdSense.

More precisely, Google offers two distinct but complementary services, concerning online advertising: AdWords (for advertisers) and AdSense (for bloggers and, in general, for website owners who want to monetize). In practice, AdSense allows the owner of a website to earn by showing ads related to products and services for which the advertisers have set specific promotional campaigns with AdWords.

AdSense provides different types of ads: link units, image ads, rich media ads, mobile ads and feed ads.

The element of greatest strength of Google AdSense is the fact that ads are characterized by a high level of contextuality respects to contents displayed in web pages.

For example, a website that deals with the world of motors, AdSense will probably display ads concerning a specific model of car or motorcycle. In contrast, in a website related to computer products, Adsense will show ads related to computer, phones, peripheral devices, etc..

About contextuality, we must emphasize that the efforts of Google for some time focus on making the ads as much as possible related to the contents of the web pages where they are shown. This allows advertisers to have a greater number of users interested, more inclined to click on banners.

Participation in the AdSense program is free and includes a series of rules that the webmaster has to respect. The most important rule is that we should never click on banner within your own website, in a fraudulent manner. This kind of action may result in the expulsion from the program, without the possibility of reintegration. In addition, other rules concerning the placement of banners and the prohibition to publish them to web pages that deal with specific topics as specified in terms and conditions.

At present, Google AdSense allows us to earn money with the contents located on the web pages of our site (AdSense for Content), in our feeds (AdSense for Feeds), into websites specifically developed for mobile phones (AdSense for Mobile), by using a specific search box installed on our site (AdSense for Search), or even by video (on YouTube).

Payments are made by check or electronic transfer funds (ETF), and the minimum payout is € 70.00. They are usually completed within 30 days from the end of the month when the amounts have been accrued.

If we don't reach the sum of at least 70 euros a month, the income achieved is maintained and added to the subsequent months, until it reaches that amount.

As with most Google services, to join AdSense, we need a Google Account. Registration can be made using the following link: http://www.google.com/adsense/.

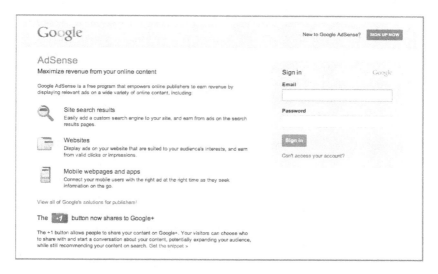

After registration, we can set up ads that we want to install on the blog.

Also for AdSense, as Analytics, we must install a script, within the HTML of our WordPress theme, in the sections where we want to show ads.

More precisely, we can insert the code directly by using the PHP editor (menu "Appearance" → "Editor"), by activating a specific widget of type "Text" and by pasting the code in it (menu "Appearance" → "Widgets"). Alternatively, if the theme is "AdSense ready", we can simply put script code or ID only within the specified options provided by theme.

The revenue, viewed through an extremely sophisticated reporting system, are usually updated with a delay of several hours.

Depending on the circumstances, AdSense can be a useful service to earn something even if our website has a few visits.

Moreover, the huge amount of dimensions and formats, for ads, the fact that we can customize the color palette and fonts to use for announcements, as well as the ability to link AdSense to other Google products like Analytics, to know the contents that generate more revenue, make it a truly unique service.

However, if you can not get from your blog at least a few thousand users per day, do not expect big earnings, most likely you will just pay you a pizza on Saturday night. Instead, if you can create a successful blog, with an adequate number of visits, then you can get a good source of income, simply by using AdSense.

Maybe, after a few months you can also get a check that is not necessarily up to 6 zeros, but a 3 or 4 yes (I think you'd like)!

Heyos

Heyos is another interesting advertising network. It has worked for over 10 years and it offers several advertising products: different formats for the banners, tooltips, pop-under, slide and dem.

Furthermore, it provides the ability to activate a type of advertising called Hotspot, which is run by Yahoo! in a similar way to AdSense ads and which requires the approval of Yahoo! itself.

Particularly interesting are the pop-under ads. Pop-under is a type of window that appears behind the browser window of a website that a user has visited.

With regard to Heyos, pop-under ads are charged to impressions (CPM). Obviously, the revenue generated are much lower compared with the PPC, but maybe it can be easier to make money by using this kind of ads, even for a blog with a few visits.

Also for Heyos, we need to install a script within the HTML of WordPress theme, in the same way of AdSense.

Heyos is able to guarantee a good degree of contextuality, lower than AdSense, but still respectable.

Payments can be made via Paypal (minimum payout: € 50.00), or via bank transfer (minimum payout: € 200.00).

Even here, in case you do not reach these amounts in a month, they are "frozen" and added to the sums earned in the following months, until they reach 50 or 200 euros.

Web sites must pass prior approval and may not cover certain topics (for example, they can't contain adult material, violence, etc.).

Registration can be made through the link: http://www.heyos.com.

Other advertising networks

In addition to AdSense and Heyos, on the Internet there are many other advertising networks based on the PPC and CPM.

Below, we list a few of them, along with some of the salient features:

BidVertiser

This is a network for PPC and CPL (Cost Per Lead) campaigns, active since 2003 and providing free participation in the program, such as AdSense and Heyos. Ads are characterized by a minor level of contextuality compared with ad networks described previously, but this probably depends on the network of advertisers, significantly smaller.

The method of payment is Paypal and the minimum amount, for payment, is $ 10.

Furthermore, it provides an internal "referral" program, which allows to earn for each advertiser or publisher registered to the service.

Website: http://www.bidvertiser.com.

Clicksor

This is also a network that manages PPC and CPM campaigns. It allows you to choose between different sizes of banners, popups, pop-unders and text links. Payment: Paypal - minimum payout: $ 5.

Website: http://www.clicksor.com.

HotPublisher

This is another network for Pay Per Click and Cost per Impression. It allows use of banners and the most common dialog boxes. I personally do not like them, but at the same time, on some websites, these boxes can be particularly effective.

Payment is by Paypal, with a payout of at least $ 50.

Website: http://hotpublisher.org.

There are many other PPC services, so many that it would be impossible to list them all.

Moreover, recently, due to the increasing use of Web sites oriented to mobile devices (smartphones, tablets, etc.), mobile advertising networks are growing more and more.

For example, if you want to create a blog that provides support for mobile devices (even with the plugin already seen in Chapter 10) you should consider to earn even through this channel. In this case, you can use an ad network like AdMob (http://www.admob.com).

In particular, AdMob was, for a long time, the undisputed leader on mobile advertising. At the end of 2009, it was acquired by Google to use its know-how and technology in conjunction with AdSense.

Currently AdMob ads are shown on all kinds of smartphones equipped with the latest operating systems (iOS, Android, Windows Phone 7, etc.).

Affiliate marketing

Another way to make money with a blog is the use of affiliate marketing. The affiliate marketing is a very powerful method to generate earnings.

However, this method requires a greater effort by the blogger and, most importantly, the ability of a typical "representative".

In practice, it works in this way: the owner of the blog uses his pages to advertise one or more products or services sold by others, obtaining a profit for every sale achieved.

The business model is the CPA (Cost per Action), where for each sale the blogger receives a commission.

Affiliations may be conducted directly between bloggers and companies that sell products and services, or by joining an affiliate network.

In the first case, the two parties negotiate directly the terms and conditions of membership and the amount of commission.

Instead, in the second case, the affiliate network acts as an intermediary, making usually available to the parties a specially crafted platform.

When the blogger joins an affiliate network (usually via subscription to an online service), he access the so-called "catalog" of affiliations, from where he can choose his preferred affiliate programs.

Unlike PPC and CPM networks, where the ads are basically managed automatically by the ad network, for affiliations the blogger decides what products or services to promote, choosing them by catalog affiliations provided by affiliate manager.

For this reason, displaying a banner is not enough to earn with affiliate networks, you have to do it in the right way, by fully exploiting your skills to choose the affiliate programs that can produce more earnings, and the best way to present them your users.

For example, imagine an affiliate network that has, within its catalog of affiliation programs, a series of products and services including:

- shoes sold by company X;
- shirts sold by different company Y;
- airline flights at extremely competitive prices, by company Z.

Well, if we run a blog concerning the fashion world, we can fill it with banners and posts about the flights offered by Company Z, but the probability that our users are interested in products and services by Company Z is very low. This is because they are interested in clothing. So, for them, affiliations relating to the sale of shoes or shirts by Companies X and Y would surely be more appropriate.

In contrast, airline flights at attractive prices may be useful in a blog concerning travels.

We said that the affiliate network make available to the affiliates a catalog of affiliate programs.

This catalog contains the list of products and services of different companies who have turned to the affiliate network for the promotion. Moreover, for each of these products or services, it shows:

- the requirements that the affiliate must meet in order to participate in each affiliate program (for example, number of site visits, topics covered, etc.);
- the type of action that users must complete, to be eligible for a commission (for example, product purchase, membership of the service, etc.);
- amount of commissions (for example: percentage of sales, fixed amount, etc.);
- type of websites that can participate in the program;
- life of "cookies" concerning the specific affiliate program.

Especially the latter factor, sometimes overlooked, can determine the success or failure in terms of earnings through affiliate systems.

Cookies are small text files used by websites to store some information on users' computers. This information, can later be read by the same websites, when users visit them again.

More precisely, in the case of affiliate programs, cookies are used to contain an affiliate code, which identifies the affiliate (in our case, the blogger) who has routed a customer to the site of the seller, through its website (blog).

Therefore, cookies are useful to allow the site that manages the affiliate program to know if a particular sale was made through a specific blog, rather than other websites.

A cookie has a lifetime. When it expires, it is no longer considered valid.

And this time interval can make difference, in terms of income, when choosing a good affiliate program.

To better describe this mechanism, let's make an example. We are browsing the blog X and we click on an affiliate link. We are directed to the sales page of the product A (a phone model that costs 200 euros). On our computer a cookie is saved for a period of 15 days.

Probably, at first glance we are interested but not willing to buy this phone. Moreover, we don't know if we have $ 200 on our rechargeable credit card, so we leave the site.

After a few days, as we are concerned that phone, we visit the website of the seller, to buy the phone. Now, if we complete the purchase within 15 days (certified by the cookie), then webmaster of blog X will earn some money. Conversely, if the purchase is concluded later, then the company that sells the phone will earn 200 euros, but the owner of the blog X will not get any money.

So, we understand that the duration of the cookie is very important for the blogger (the affiliate) and it should be as long as possible, in relation to the type of treated product or service.

On the Internet there are numerous affiliate networks. The most important are:

- TradeDoubler (http://www.tradedoubler.com);

- Zanox (http://www.zanox.com);
- Commission Junction (http://www.cj.com);
- Kontera (http://www.kontera.com);
- Sprintrade (http://www.sprintrade.com).

The direct sale of banners and links

Some people do not want to depend on affiliate or advertising network, to obtain earnings from their own blog.

In these cases, an alternative may be represented by direct selling of banner space and / or text links within the blog.

However, often a blogger who chooses this option is forced to invest much time, both for the creation of contents of his blog, and to search for potential buyers of web spaces available.

Moreover, as often happens also in other contexts, people ready to pay hundreds or even thousands of dollars for advertising on AdWords, are not as well inclined to pay a blogger who wants to sell a web space for a few tens of euros, for a banner displayed for 30 days.

All this involves a considerable effort for the blogger, that can incur in delusions and lengthy negotiations, with negative consequences about enthusiasm.

For this reason, my personal recommendation is to use more than one system, especially at the beginning of a new experience as blogger and when you cannot rely on a large number of visitors.

At a later time, as the blog will grow and will be able to get a good number of daily visits, you can also consider the direct sale of spaces and, eventually, publishing of sponsored posts.

Concluding remarks

Dear Reader,

first, thank you for reading this book.

I hope that thanks to the information contained in it, you're already able to create your own blog and to taste a bit of its "magic".

If you found that this book was interesting, please, let me know it.

You can contact me by using my blog SPACE 4 TUTORIAL (http://www.space4tutorial.com - a random blog. I developed many other blogs, but this was my first blog and I am bound to it in a special way), or my new website TRAVAGLIANTE (http://www.travagliante.com).

And, of course, do not hesitate to speak of this book to your friends and relatives.

Also, if you have suggestions about further information to add in these pages, or if you wish to report me any mistake, do not hesitate to contact me. In other words, let me know your point of view.

Throughout this book, we were able to address different aspects regarding the management of a blog.

If you have not yet tried to create your own blog, then I suggest you "do it now!", because only blogging, you will realize how this activity can be fascinating.

Whether you do it for your own personal satisfaction, or to promote your business, or even to earn money through the different methods of advertising, you must know that the passion for the blog will take you to discover a fantastic world, rich in new ideas and new inputs, where you can also establish relationships with people who have "much to give you".

In these pages we have said that, when you must choose your own "niche", you should prefer topics that you know.

With respect, I also suggest one thing: write what you know, but especially about topics that interest you and fascinate you! Be careful, because the two do not always coincide!

In fact, if you don't like very well the topics that you know, then after a while you will get tired and the failure will be assured.

Instead, if you create a blog about a topic that fascinates you, then you will be encouraged to deepen, possibly to study, grow, and it will be easier to turn your blog into a solid point of reference, in the blogosphere.

Another hint: the blog is based on the concepts of "sharing" and "participation". If you want that your blog is a participated blog, then you must be the first person to participate in discussions available on other blogs. In this way, the other bloggers, along with their users, will have the opportunity to meet you, to know what are your opinions and your points of view.

So, you can be appreciated and you can forge relationships that will have positive consequences, possibly from a professional perspective. In this sense, remember that, sometimes, thanks to collaboration between several bloggers, important projects were born (with enormous satisfaction in terms of personal and economic).

I would say so much more, to better illustrate the beauty of blogging, but I think that nothing can be more effective than trying immediately to create a blog and start writing.

Therefore, I stop here, and I warn you that a blog can grow and become a successful blog only if you have the right love and passion. And it can become a great tool to better express your creativity.

Good luck with your blog! And please, let me know how it will be!

Roberto Travagliante

Credits

In this section I wish to report my personal thanks to all those who, consciously or unconsciously, have made sure that this book was made.

Usually, in these pages an author thanks the persons who have contributed to the realization of a book. These persons are often linked to the author by a professional relationship (for example, here you can find names of employees of an editor, all who planned the correction, or all who have shown their effort in writing of certain parts, and so on).

Since this book is self-produced, this type of thanks there will not be.

There are, instead, the "THANKS" I feel I have to tell people that, in one way or another, with their behavior, have encouraged the writing of "WordPress from A to W".

I'm not an expert on the "chaos theory", but sometimes, when I retrace certain events occurred, I am reminded of an expression of Edward Norton Lorenz, that encapsulates the neologism butterfly effect, and that states:

"does the flap of a butterfly's wings in Brazil
set off a tornado in Texas?"

And, when I think about the sequence of the various events that influenced my choices so far, I realize that without the inputs received by some people, probably today not only I would not made this book, but I would not mind even computer.

For this reason, the first person I want to thank is my father. His main merit is that he brought home, now almost 25 years ago, a Commodore VIC 20. Thanks to him we savored, both me and my little brother, the charm of technology. In 1988, for an 8 year old boy like me, that thing was too special to pass unnoticed.

Me and Daniele, my brother, spent whole evenings with that object which appeared almost "magical" to our eyes. As long as my father (seeing us for too long committed to overcoming the various levels of the game "Omega Race") told us that the computer was not to be used only to waste time, but also to do more useful things.

During the same day, he took out a practical guide about the BASIC language and I thought "if I learn to develop programs, then I can create games that I like".

My father may not know it, but from there it all started. More and more passion for computing has grown in me, with specific interest in computer programming.

Especially in this phase, my mother was decisive. So, thank you mum! Because worrying about the fact that I spent time at the computer, you taught me to find the right balance between this and other activities that would normally affect a child. All of this, with the love that only a mother can give.

The other persons I would like to thank are Federico Pietro Crotti and Christian Sassano.

Thank you, Federico, for your valuable suggestions received on several occasions, especially those relating to the practical aspects on publishing of a book or an ebook.

And thank you, Christian, colleague and friend (and excellent graphics expert), for the cover of this book, made with good taste, great professionalism and with a precision almost "obsessive". Thank you also for the suggested title of this book, which enables one to perceive the essence of it in the way I wanted.

Finally, my special thanks is for the two most important women in my life: Miriam and Maria Teresa. This book is dedicated to you.

You, Miriam, my sweet princess of two years, you have obtained the merit to put me to bed, many nights, when the unique alternative was to work late for writing this book.

In fact, under the pretext of going to sleep with your dad, many times you've convinced me to go to sleep, leaving everything to the next day.

Instead, Maria Teresa, my wife, thank you for support me whenever I undertake a new project. Thanks for bearing with me during every phase of this writing. Thanks for your relevant suggestions about production of a book that would address all aspects necessary to achieve a blog.

What I appreciate is your ability to not only satisfy my choices, but to push further, often proposing winning ideas and participating actively in all that concerns our passions and interests.

You do not know it, but when I think of the ideal life partner, I think of you.